Faith Meets World

The Gift and Challenge
of Catholic Social Teaching

Faith MEETS World

The Gift and Challenge of Catholic Social Teaching

Barry Hudock

Liguori
LIGUORI, MISSOURI

Imprimi Potest:
Harry Grile, CSsR, Provincial
Denver Province, The Redemptorists

Published by Liguori Publications
Liguori, Missouri 63057

To order, call 800-325-9521
www.liguori.org

Library of Congress Cataloging-in-Publication Data

Hudock, Barry.
Faith meets world : the gift and challenge of Catholic social teaching / Barry Hudock.
 p. cm
1. Christian sociology—Catholic Church. I. Title.
 BX1753. H75 2013
 261.088'282—dc23
 2012044126
 p ISBN 978-0-7648-2224-7
 e ISBN 978-0-7648-2303-9

Liguori Publications, a nonprofit corporation, is an apostolate of The Redemptorists. To learn more about The Redemptorists, visit Redemptorists.com.

Printed in the United States of America
17 16 15 14 13 / 5 4 3 2 1
First Edition

Contents

Dedication

This book is dedicated to the people of Mingo County, West Virginia,

with mountains of affection, esteem, and gratitude.

That goes especially for Sister Brendan Conlon, OSU,

and Sister Janet Peterworth, OSU, heroes both.

And to my brother, Marc, who asked the question.

Acknowledgments

Regarding the genesis and preparation of this book, I am grateful for various reasons and in various ways to:

the students, staff, and administration of Christian Brothers Academy in Syracuse, New York, and particularly to Marilyn Goulet for many good conversations in the car on the way to work and for the compelling witness of her own life;

everyone associated with Christian Help of Mingo County and ABLE Families, including the boards of directors and founding executive directors of the two agencies who brought me there, and the people of Mingo County, West Virginia, and Martin County, Kentucky;

my wife, Toni, who is still my treasure and a fellow traveler on the journey;

our children, Abigail, Cecilia, Nicholas, Hope, Gianna, Jacob, and Brittany, who are willing to put up with the fact that Dad is still not writing a novel for kids;

the professional, creative, and faith-filled staff at Liguori Publications, who have been a pleasure to work with and who have lived up to their mission, vision, and heritage.

Thank you, all.

Visit the blog:
barryhudock.wordpress.com

Introduction

"[H]ave we so domesticated and trivialized our Christian commitment, our devotion to Jesus himself, that we look on him simply as someone to...provide us with comforting religious experiences?"

Anglican scholar and bishop N.T. Wright is asking the question, and if you're like me, it makes you squirm. We squirm because we both know, you and I, in our best and most honest moments, that authentic Christian faith is not only comforting but also terribly challenging. Part of the challenge is the way a relationship with Jesus and an engagement with the gospel compels us to be effectively and lovingly engaged in the world around us.

This engagement with the world is the subject of Catholic Social Teaching. (We'll call it CST for short in this book.) CST is both a gift and a challenge. It's a gift because it offers a life-giving vision that we know in our bones describes who we were made to be and how we were made to live. It's a challenge because its implications are difficult, demanding, and inconvenient to many of our closely held presumptions.

Maybe it's too challenging even for those who lead the Church and teach the Catholic faith because we've done a pretty good job of keeping a lid on it. For the most part, even many committed Catholics have been largely unaware of the Church's vision for society. Good folks who could explain the theological intricacies of transubstantiation, the Immaculate Conception, and infallibility sometimes struggle even to recognize the universal destination of goods or subsidiarity as Catholic terms.

In some fascinating ways, the American presidential election of 2012 may have helped change that. In response to positions taken and comments made by Catholic politicians, CST was explained and debated vigorously by *The Wall Street Journal, Slate, The Huffington Post,* and in online comment boxes and discussion forums across the Internet. With that election now history, the media and inside-the-beltway operatives have moved on to other things. They were never all that interested in the doctrine anyway, but only in the political points that could be won or lost by arguing over it.

My hope is that the Catholic community can now take a breath and continue, outside the glare of spotlights, a good and healthy conversation about CST, why it makes sense, and what it should mean to our lives together. That, in part, is the reason for this book—to keep the conversation going, because it's a conversation we need to have.

Don't get me wrong: We are not talking politics here—or at any rate, not primarily politics. We're talking about the Gospel of Jesus Christ, the Good News that God offers to humanity about who God is, who we are, how we relate to God, and what that relationship means. It has been the task and joy of Christians from the beginning to grasp that news ever more deeply and make it known to a world that badly needs to hear it.

For half a century now, popes have insisted that we must renew our commitment to this task, even speaking of a need for a New Evangelization—one that is new in its methods, its ardor, and its expression (as Pope John Paul II described it). And each of them has insisted, one after another, that *the social mission of the Church is an essential part of its message.*

"The 'new evangelization,' which the modern world urgently needs and which I have emphasized many times, must include among its essential elements a proclamation of the Church's social doctrine," wrote John Paul II. Paul VI before him and Benedict XVI after him expressed similar convictions.

So this is not about which party we belong to, not about being liberal or conservative. For Catholics, this is about being a person and also about being Catholic. It's about being the person God calls us to be in the society that God wants us to have.

Be careful, though. In the 1930s, Catholic Worker cofounder Peter Maurin called this stuff "the dynamite of the Church." He used explosive imagery for a reason. There's bang to this message. It has a kick. Paul VI talked about "upsetting, through the power of the gospel, mankind's criteria of judgment." And people don't like their criteria of judgment upset. I know I don't. So like every other effort at evangelization we make, we must do it with patience and love. There is no place in this for anger or combativeness. No one is always right, and that includes the ways we understand and explain the content of doctrinal teaching. I've tried to remember that as I've prepared these words, and I hope those who consider and discuss them will, too.

***

I want to mention a problem I faced in writing this book, because I realized early on that whatever solution I chose was bound to leave some readers unsatisfied. The Church presents its teaching in the form of doctrinal statements—documents, catechisms, and the like. In the case of CST, that primarily means papal encyclicals, which I'll explain a bit in chapter 1. For now, suffice it to say that papal encyclicals have a style all their own, and that's putting it kindly. They are usually dense, wordy, abstract, and formal. In a sense, their purpose and their intended readership demands it. But the result is that they rarely make for easy or inspiring reading for anyone but the most committed and enthusiastic readers.

In the interest of presenting this book in a style that is readable and engaging, I've tried to avoid too much quoting from these encyclicals and other Church documents. This has felt like a handicap at times. I've shaken my head at the idea of trying to write a book about CST without quoting CST. But I've worked hard at paraphrasing and illustrating in ways that are both accurate and faithful to the thinking of the popes who wrote them. Of course, there are times when an exact quotation is most helpful and clear.

Some readers, however, will want to know exactly where these teachings are found in the encyclicals and exactly how they are worded. Where personal convictions are challenged (or criteria of judgment upset), some may understandably approach these ideas with suspicion and want verification that I'm not twisting the teachings or providing my own personal spin. Fair enough. For those who want to check references, read the original teaching in full, or read more deeply on a given topic, the suggestions for further reading provide citations and suggestions.

***

Finally, throughout my work on this project, a bigger problem has been frequently on my mind, and that is the inadequacy with which I have lived out these teachings myself. Anyone who tries to talk about these demanding doctrines always risks making himself or herself a hypocrite.

I have taken some comfort and inspiration in words written by Dorothy Day—the other cofounder of the Catholic Worker movement and an American hero of CST—in her personal diary during the summer of 1953: "I speak and write so much better than I perform. But we can never lower the ideal because we fail in living up to it."

PART ONE

Getting to Know Catholic Social Teaching

Chapter 1

What Is Catholic Social Teaching?

A high school athlete stops in the midst of a state championship race to help a collapsed opponent struggle across the finish line. A man runs into a burning house to save an elderly neighbor. An Olympic champion sells her medal to help pay the medical expenses of a sick child.

We know goodness when we see it, don't we? Like me, you're surely struck with admiration when you hear the stories of Meghan Vogel, Jeremie Wentworth, and Zofia Noceti-Klepacka. (A quick Internet search will offer you more information about each of them.) We know what it means to do the right thing, and we recognize it in action.

We know evil, too, in versions big and small, though we're sometimes uncomfortable calling it that. A woman raped in a neighborhood park. An airline ignoring safety procedures for the sake of profit. Children at play in a back yard, belittling and humiliating the smallest one among them.

Doing good and avoiding evil are important parts of being the people God created us to be. But not all choices, not all moral issues, are individual ones. Actually, in a very real way, none are (as the examples above demonstrate well). But some have a profoundly social character to them. The ways we choose to structure our society through business, finance, politics, government, and more—these, too, are issues with serious moral elements.

If Christian morality is about what it means to be and to authentically live as a human person, CST is about living together as persons in society.

Where do these teachings come from? The Church identifies two paths to moral truth available to us. They are closely connected. In fact, they are simply two ways God communicates with humanity about the kind of people we are made to be. These paths are reason and revelation.

Natural law

After World War II, many Nazi leaders were tried and convicted at the famous Nuremberg Trials. Grave sentences were handed down to Hermann Goering, Rudolf Hess, Hans Frank, and others responsible for the atrocities of the Holocaust. Yet most of these atrocities were completely legal at the time they were committed. The Nazi party had crafted the laws that permitted what they wanted to do. At Nuremberg, Nazi leaders were convicted of "crimes against humanity" and "crimes against peace," terms that were created for the purpose of the trial.

How can a person be convicted of breaking a law that was not in effect when they acted? Most of the time, they can't. But in this case, the international court recognized that there are some things that any person is able to understand to be gravely wrong, regardless of what the law says. With our reasoning, each person is able to reflect on human experience, learn from it, and draw conclusions about morality. Moral standards are derived from the very nature of what it means to be human. These standards are called natural law.

Natural law is not simply "what we do naturally." It's "natural" for us to become jealous of one another, angry with one another, even violent with one another. But these are not demonstrations of natural law. Natural law is what serves our well-being best, what we should do in order most truly to flourish as persons. It is our moral common sense. Because human nature is universal, so is natural law.

Not everyone agrees with this. (The philosopher Thomas Hobbes, for example, saw our human laws as nothing more than what the lawmaker wants, so there can be no "unjust law.") But everyone lives as though we're certain natural law is real. If someone steals my car, I don't wonder if that person was perhaps from a culture where taking someone else's car is a good moral choice. I want the thief found and my car returned! If a neighborhood bully has been picking on my daughter at the playground, I don't think that perhaps the other child has a different and equally valid value system; I know something needs to be done and the bullying must stop.

The Declaration of Independence cites natural law when it speaks of truths that are "self-evident" and rights that are "unalienable." Martin Luther King, Jr., referred to natural law as a keystone of the civil rights movement, citing it as the reason that not all human laws are just laws and that unjust laws must be rejected and changed.

The Nuremberg judges, the authors of the Declaration, and Dr. King all shared a confidence in human reason, in the fact that one need not be Christian or the citizen of a certain nation to sort out important moral questions. The same confidence has allowed the Church to engage the secular world in important issues related to the good of the human community. The popes can talk about human dignity, human rights, and the common good, knowing that everyone can understand them and their value to us as persons. They can address their encyclicals not only to the faithful members of their own flock, but to "all people of good will."

Divine revelation

A second way we come to understand moral truth is by divine revelation—God's revelation of God's self and God's plan of love, goodness, and salvation for humanity. This revelation has been carried out in stages. It happened when God entered into a covenant with Noah, when God chose Abraham and Sarah to form a family that would become a great people, and when God led that people out of slavery into a new land of promise. In Jesus, it reached its culmination and its fullness.

God's revelation is transmitted through sacred Scripture and sacred tradition. Because interpreting it and its meaning to us is not always a simple matter (as Church history makes obvious), he provides the magisterium of the Church (the teaching of the pope, bishops, and councils) as an authoritative guide. The magisterium does not control revelation, and it is not superior to the Scriptures or tradition that transmit it to us. Rather, it serves, listens to, guards, and proclaims the content of revelation.

Popes, bishops, and councils convey their teachings through letters and documents that vary in importance and doctrinal weight. Among the weightiest, at least in recent centuries, are papal encyclicals. As we'll see, these documents have an important place in the formation of modern CST.

Not all revelation is about morality, but some of it is. (The *Catechism of the Catholic Church*, a summary of all Church teaching, has four major parts: on the creed, the sacraments, the moral life, and prayer.) CST is one aspect of the Church's magisterium, and it falls under the broader category of morality. Like the rest of the teachings of the magisterium, it is rooted in Scripture and sacred tradition. Like the rest of its moral teachings, the Church believes that CST is also accessible through the natural law.

Living out Jesus' commandment to love one another in the context of society is what CST is all about. Pope Benedict XVI writes, "To love someone is to desire that person's good and to take effective steps to secure it. Besides the good of the individual, there is a good that is linked to living in society: the common good. It is the good of 'all of us,' made up of individuals, families, and intermediate groups who together constitute society."

What CST is not

That's not to say that CST offers a clear and ready answer to every question we have about our lives together. God's revelation is not a list of policy guidelines and economic regulations. Sometimes the answers to problems are not absolutely clear, and certainty about them is difficult or even impossible to reach.

What constitutes a just wage for a worker or fair price for a product? Can a nuclear bomb ever be used in a moral way? How can energy providers operate their businesses in ways that allow them to both earn a profit and respect the environment? The questions go on and on. Very often, CST provides principles that help talented people come up with good answers; it does not provide them all ready-made. It is up to individual believers to make the best decisions they can—prudential judgments—about how best to apply the principles to real life.

Of course, making space for prudential judgment also introduces the opportunity for any of us fudge things a bit, to twist the principles into something they are not in order to justify conclusions we're partial to. Employers, for example, must certainly use prudential judgment in making decisions about workplace policies and how they deal with employees; that's far from saying that whatever an employer chooses to do is right or morally acceptable. Some prudential judgments are simply wrong ones. How the principles of CST are applied in specific situations are often open to our personal judgment, but for the faithful Catholic, whether they must be applied is not. The point of CST is not to get the Church's doctrines transferred into civil laws. The Church is not out to establish a theocracy based on doctrines revealed by God. But civil laws, policies, institutions, and social attitudes all reflect moral judgments about what it means to be a person in society. The Church is convinced that both reason and revelation tell us something important about that.

And so it seeks, says the *Compendium of the Social Doctrine of the Church*, "to proclaim the Gospel in the context of society, to make the liberating word of the Gospel resound in the complex worlds of production, labour, business, finance, trade, politics, law, culture, social communications, where men and women live....Because of the public relevance of the Gospel and faith, because of the corrupting effects of injustice, that is, of sin, the Church cannot remain indifferent to social matters."

As we'll see in the chapters ahead, at the heart of this gospel vision is human dignity and solidarity. When you take human dignity and solidarity seriously, you end up with human rights and the common good. When you apply human rights and the common good to lived reality, you find the universal destination of goods, preferential option for the poor, and subsidiarity. Some of the real-life contexts and circumstances in which all of this must be applied is within family life, work, the economy, politics, the environment, decisions related to peace and war, and some major social issues related to life and death. That is the path this book will follow.

Along the way, we will discover what Archbishop Óscar Romero called "the beautiful but harsh truth that the Christian faith does not cut us off from the world but immerses us in it." Beautiful and harsh, CST presents both a gift and a challenge. If, at any point, either of these two sides of CST don't seem to be quite the case, then there is surely something more about it left to be learned.

Chapter 2

What Mr. Newcomen Started
(Backstory I)

The middle-aged single man who made his living dealing in iron and hardware in the small harbor town would never have believed he was about to set off the most significant shift in human society in 10,000 years. But that's what happened.

Introducing the Industrial Revolution

At the beginning of the eighteenth century, the landscape around Dartmouth, England, was dotted by tin mines, and Thomas Newcomen heard a lot of complaining from the mine owners about the almost constant slow flooding of the mines. Pumping the water out manually or hauling it into large buckets pulled by horses was slow, difficult, and meant much lost income.

Newcomen came up with a better way. He devised an engine powered by the force of the pressure created by condensing steam. It was 1712, and thanks to this innovator, the steam engine was born. Soon Newcomen's steam engine was being used throughout England and the rest of Europe—and for the first time, machines were doing work previously accomplished by men or horses, more quickly and for less cost!

Similar British inventions followed. There was a water-powered spinning machine that revolutionized the textile industry. That machine's creator built several, put up a building to house his machines, and hired workers to keep them running and producing at a constant pace (more production means more profit). The factory was born.

Another new machine efficiently rolled out hot lumps of molten metal into bars, eliminating the need for them to be hammered into shape one by one. It's a history with plenty of fascinating details, but you get the picture.

The changes that the Industrial Revolution brought are massive. It marks:

- the beginning of a market economy;

- the movement of populations from countrysides to cities for the promise of jobs (a movement which has continued to this day: the year 2007 marked the first time in human history that a majority of the world's population lived in cities rather than rural areas);

- the beginning of life lived according to the rhythms of a time clock rather than through nature's sunrises, sunsets, and seasons;

- an entirely new and sweeping division of people within society: those who owned the means of production and the profits that came from selling what was produced on one hand, and those who worked for pay to use those means to make things on the other.

In short, it represents perhaps the most significant development in human society since the invention of agriculture 10,000 years earlier, when our hunter-gatherer ancestors learned to live in one place by growing food in an organized way.

In many ways, this was good—very good! The Industrial Revolution introduced all kinds of previously unimaginable opportunities, advances, productivity, professions, products, conveniences, and yes, wealth. It would be dishonest and a bit crazy not to acknowledge the enormous boon to Western society that the Industrial Revolution has been, right up to today.

But the blessings did not come without serious curses. The flood of job-seekers flowing into the cities meant fewer jobs than workers. This gave the owners of factories great power. They could hire desperate people at very low wages. Those low-paid workers, in order to survive, were willing to work very long hours, with few breaks or days off. Owners didn't bother making sure the factories were safe or clean. When a man's pay could not support his family, his wife and children took jobs, too, in similar unsafe and unclean places. These new city-dwellers ended up crowding together in cramped and unsanitary conditions. It was a degrading and miserable way to live, and millions of people in the Western world were suddenly living it.

A first significant reaction to these conditions was the birth of Marxist socialism. Karl Marx, a Russian living in England at the time, observed the squalor with anguish. From his frustration and reflection on the situation, he proposed an alternative, one in which workers united to demand that their dignity be respected, and where no one held power over others because they owned more. Marx's Communist Manifesto (1848) sounded good to many who read it or heard its ideas.

Pope Leo speaks

Marxism was one major response to the new social circumstances. In 1891, Pope Leo XIII offered another, with the publication of the encyclical *Rerum Novarum* (On the Condition of the Working Class, or On Capital and Labor). The very title of the encyclical (which means literally "of new things," from the Latin of the very first sentence) implies that something new was happening within the Church in response to the new circumstances of society, and indeed it was.

Leo opened his letter by pointing to "the misery and wretchedness pressing so unjustly on the majority of the working class." He complained that "working men have been surrendered, isolated and helpless, to the hardheartedness of employers and the greed of unchecked competition" and that "a small number of very rich men have been able to lay upon the teeming masses of the laboring poor a yoke little better than that of slavery itself."

The heart of *Rerum Novarum* is Leo's insistence that workers are not simply instruments to be bought and used by those who employ them, like someone might purchase a tool and use it as he pleases. Leo insisted that the willingness of people desperate for income to accept a low wage did not make paying such a wage morally right. In fact, he argued, employers had a duty to pay wages that allowed a man (a husband was the presumed head of a household) to provide a reasonable living for his family.

Leo went on to insist on a worker's right to organize in unions. The American cardinal, James Gibbons, archbishop of Baltimore, had played an important behind-the-scenes role in Leo's thinking on that topic. For Leo, though, unchecked capitalism was not the only threat to the well-being of people and society; socialism brought problems of its own. He defended at great length the right to private property and said that preserving this right was an important part of the solution to the poverty of many. Leo also rejected Marxism's view of history as an inevitable struggle between the classes. Another important aspect of Leo's encyclical was the conviction that people might be poor for reasons other than their own laziness, that the society around them might push them into poverty or prevent them from getting out of it. As we will see, this idea has affected CST and how it is lived out in major ways.

Rooted in revelation

And so it began. Modern Catholic Social Teaching was born. But let's be clear. The circumstances Leo addressed were new, and his encyclical marks the beginning of a new era in Church teaching. But in some ways what Leo had to say was very, very old. The moral principles that undergirded Leo's teaching would be recognized by believers throughout Christian history and, even farther back, by the Israelite people who entered into the first covenant with God.

The creation stories of the Old Testament make clear in striking ways the beauty and goodness of the entire created world, the fundamental dignity of every human person, and the unity and basic equality that all people share. The historical books of the Old Testament present a narrative in which God stands on the side of a poor and oppressed people (crying out through Moses, "Let my people go!") in their struggle with a powerful empire that works hard to keep them down. One of the central messages of the prophets, like Isaiah, Jeremiah, Amos, and Micah, is that God demands justice, peace, and care for the poor among the people of the covenant.

The gospels depict a Jesus who stood dramatically with the poor and proclaimed that his kingdom was theirs, and he had some hard-edged things to say to and about the rich. Jesus made clear that being his disciple was not only about assenting to certain truths but about living a way of life, and central to that way was living in peace, solidarity, and justice while renouncing the use of power or violence to take advantage of others.

Elsewhere in the New Testament, the Apostle Paul berated one early Christian community, insisting that the Eucharists where the rich ate and drank ahead of and more than the poor were hardly Eucharists at all (1 Corinthians 11:17–22), and John bluntly questioned whether the love of God can possibly remain in those who have money when they refuse to use it to help those who are in need (1 John 3:11–18). James, looking forward to the coming of the Lord in glory, has unsettling things to say about "impending miseries" for those who are rich (James 5:1–7)—and those who withhold wages from workers receive a special mention (v. 4).

As Christianity grew through its early years, these teachings and this way of life was expressed in the writings and homilies of the Fathers of the Church. They're expressed too in the work of great medieval theologians, most especially the thirteenth century's Saint Thomas Aquinas, who stands far above the rest in stature. In fact, Thomas' thinking is foundational in modern CST not only because his work in theology and philosophy is such an incredible achievement, but because Pope Leo, who initiated modern CST with *Rerum Novarum*, also spurred a great resurgence of interest in Thomas' thought and insisted that all good theology is rooted in it. Thanks to Leo, a vibrant "neo-scholasticism" took root alongside CST, nourished it, and was ultimately outlived by it. Many ideas prominent in Thomas' work find an important place in modern CST, including natural law, the natural role of the state in human society, the central place of the virtue of justice, and even the just-war tradition.

In the sixteenth century, in the wake of the Protestant Reformation, many Catholics found new and important ways to live out their convictions, including through several new religious orders that provided heroic service to the poor and marginalized of society. These include Saint Angela Merici's Ursuline sisters, Saint Francis de Sales' and Saint Frances de Chantal's Sisters of the Visitation, and Saint Vincent de Paul's Sisters of Charity. They represent an army of Christian compassion that mobilized in some groundbreaking ways and whose spiritual offspring continue marching today.

"With the entrails of the last priest"

Roughly a century after the Reformation took hold—and perhaps as a result of the Reformation—the Enlightenment was born. This intellectual and cultural movement began what historians call "the Age of Reason" because it insisted on complete and exclusive trust in the power of human reason to solve problems and fuel progress of all kinds. Science was considered the supremely important field of study, because it is based solely on what can be observed and measured. Any ideas not founded strictly upon reason were judged to be opposed to reason and rejected with contempt. Ideas or practices that were traditional were discarded because they were traditional. Divine revelation? Preposterous! Miracles? Nonsense! Metaphysics? Superstition! And Church authority? Be damned!

To leaders of this movement, the Catholic Church was seen as the ultimate enemy of all that was good and right. The famous writer Voltaire (1694–1778) vilified the Church relentlessly in a long series of essays, histories, novels, and plays. The philosopher Denis Diderot (1713–1784), who ranks second only to Voltaire as hero of the movement, summarized the thinking well: "Man will never be free until the last king is strangled with the entrails of the last priest."

That's not to say that the Enlightenment was a pure disaster, even from a Catholic perspective today. Many ideas about freedom, equality, and democracy were encouraged and grew strong in the very same environment. In fact, the American Revolution and its expression in the Declaration of Independence is a dramatic fruit of Enlightenment thinking.

Most Church leaders took a strongly defensive stance, rejecting and condemning just about all of it, including the parts about freedom, equality, and democracy, despite the fact that these ideas too are rooted in Christian revelation. Two centuries later, it's difficult to understand this. But before about 1700, pretty much everyone in the Western world had a very paternalistic and hierarchical view of society and how it was to be governed. Most people truly were illiterate, uneducated, and poor; a person of power to guide, protect, and defend them was largely a good thing. That was the role of the monarchy. Since things had been this way for centuries, and the very limited historical sense of the time allowed people to think it had just about always been so, this was understood by some as God's own plan for humanity. And so, along with condemnations of all the new secular, anti-religious thinking, the Church also condemned the new ideas of individual freedom, the equality of all people, and the right of people to speak out and participate in their own government. Though some important Catholic thinking about human rights and freedoms went on in previous centuries, the papacy's response to the Enlightenment quashed all that.

The culmination of this approach came in 1864, with Pope Pius IX's encyclical *Quanta Cura* and its famous appendix, the *Syllabus of Errors*. The Pope offered a long list of "errors" of the day that included the separation of church and state, free speech, freedom of conscience, freedom of the press, and freedom of religion. He capped it off with the utter rejection of the idea that "the Roman Pontiff can and ought to reconcile himself and reach agreement with progress, liberalism, and modern civilization." (Interestingly, as we'll see, the papacy and the Church it led would, in the span of just a century, move from complete rejection of these ideas to becoming one of the world's foremost defenders of several them.)

This takes us up to the eve of Pope Leo's *Rerum Novarum* in 1891. But the publication of this encyclical only marks the beginning. A dramatic new era of the Church's engagement with the world had begun.

Chapter 3

Hammered Out in History
(Backstory II)

Though we don't have the room here to study each stage in the history of modern CST in great detail, a quick stroll through the story is certainly helpful in understanding what it is and how it came to be. As the decades rolled on, they brought a series of important developments in the way peoples and nations live together. At every point, the Church has sought to apply the principles of CST to the circumstances in which we find ourselves.

At the end of the 1920s the Great Depression struck the West. (And yes, much of CST, especially during the first century of its development, has focused on life in Western society—that is, primarily western Europe and the United States—and has often given the impression that the Church has not realized there are other places, cultures, and circumstances in the world.) The economies of the United States and Europe were devastated, and the movements of fascism and communism were on the rise.

Pope Pius XI responded with an encyclical called *Quadragesimo Anno* (1931). He restated in strong terms the Church's support of workers and their right to just wages, and he condemned the divisions and the gap between the rich and the poor. He sought to advance the kingdom of Christ by bringing about a just social order that rejected both capitalism's relentless competition and communism's violent rejection of both private property and of God. He proposed a society based not on the market and not on the state, but on the various functions that people carry out in society. Rather than being divided between owners and workers, those who work in the same profession or trade

29

should be united in corporate groups. (It was a dramatic proposition that ultimately would come to nothing and be mostly ignored, even by his own successors.) This important encyclical introduced the term "social justice" to the Catholic vocabulary.

In the 1940s came the Second World War, and in its aftermath, society again shifted and developed. An awareness of the reality and legitimacy of other cultures in the world grew. The Cold War between the Communist bloc nations and Western democracies began, introducing troubling new threats to humanity. Pope John XXIII responded with the encyclical *Mater et Magistra* (1961), emphasizing global interdependence and introducing the issue of developing nations, and then with *Pacem in Terris* (1963), on world peace through human rights.

Responding to the rapidly changing society in which the Church found itself was also the reason for Pope John's historic decision to convoke the bishops of the globe for the Second Vatican Council (1962–1965). The fruit of these bishops' deliberations was sixteen documents of varying authority and importance, two of which deal directly with issues of CST. The council's Pastoral Constitution on the Church in the Modern World, *Gaudium et Spes* (1965), explores CST in some dramatic ways, emphasizing the Church's commitment to promoting human dignity. The Declaration on Religious Freedom, *Dignitatis Humanae* (1965), focused on the relationship between the Church and the state in an approach that owed much to the American theologian John Courtney Murray.

As the twentieth century progressed, important developments in science, technology, and communications brought a faster pace to life, new opportunities, incredible new knowledge and capacities, and also wealth previously unseen by most people on the planet. Modern communications made us aware of the terrible poverty in which much of humanity lived and the huge gap between resources available to the rich and the poor people of the planet. Pope Paul VI published *Populorum Progressio* (1967), a historic encyclical on human development, emphasizing the universal destination of goods we'll consider in chapter 8. By proposing the idea of integral human development, he insisted that economic well-being is one thing, and an essential thing, but not the only thing; in fact, without the other things (personal, spiritual, moral, cultural, social development) it can hurt.

Paul VI chose to mark the eightieth anniversary of *Rerum Novarum* with a special apostolic letter to Maurice Cardinal Roy, president of the Pontifical Commission on Peace and Justice. Titled *Octogesima Adveniens* (1971), the letter emphasizes the importance of politics, rather than economics, in the struggle for justice. It includes several "firsts" for a papal document: a first expression of serious concern about the environment, a first exploration of the problems and dangers of urbanization, and a first major reference by a pope to the "preferential respect due to the poor and the special situation they have in society" that we will explore later. The letter is also unique for its acknowledgment that the diversity of situations and cultures around the world means that the pope often cannot provide answers to issues and problems that are valid always and everywhere. Rather, local Christian communities must reflect on their own situations in the light of the gospel and come up with their own solutions.

The passing of years also brought continuing development in the world of work, including the impact of technology, the arrival of great multinational corporations, and also the growing influence of communism. In this context, Pope John Paul II offered *Laborem Exercens* (1982), a historic reflection on the rights of workers, solidarity, and a theology of work.

Meanwhile, ever-improving communications shed an increasingly brighter light on the desperate poverty of many "underdeveloped" nations on the planet, while the gap between the rich and poor nations (as well as between rich and poor people within nations) only grew wider. John Paul II marked the twentieth anniversary of *Populorum Progressio* with *Sollicitudo Rei Socialis* (1987), a major statement on human development and human solidarity. The Pope recognized that many people and nations remain poor not simply because they are "underdeveloped," as though they simply have not been able to keep up with other more fortunate ones, but because of unjust social structures that conspire to keep them poor. He also offered a strong critique of the rampant consumerism of Western nations.

The year 1989 brought dramatic changes to global politics and economics with the mostly nonviolent fall of the Soviet Union. On the centenary of *Rerum Novarum*, John Paul II offered *Centesimus Annus* (1991), an encyclical which offers a guarded affirmation of the market economy, insisting it must be regulated to protect the poor, and of capitalism in the sense of a positive role of business and private property, but not in the sense of economic freedom being supreme and unregulated.

The Pope raised another strong warning about a dangerous social reality in the publication of his encyclical, *Evangelium Vitae* (1995). In the face of what seemed to be increasingly pervasive disregard for human life itself, manifested in a developing "culture of death," John Paul II insisted on the sanctity and the inviolable dignity of every human life. He offered strong, authoritative statements about the immorality of the taking of any innocent human life, of abortion, and of euthanasia, and he insisted that the circumstances in which the death penalty might morally be used are all but nonexistent in the modern world.

Pope Benedict XVI had chosen to mark the fortieth anniversary of *Populorum Progressio* in 2007. But in an excellent demonstration of the Church's desire to address current realities in its social teaching, the Pope, noting the onset of the global financial crisis in the middle of that year and the great recession which followed upon it, chose to wait, observe, and reflect on the circumstances of the day. In June of 2009, he published *Caritas in Veritate*, a bold and innovative reassessment of global economics and exploration of the theological foundations of both the market and government. But, as many commentators noted, it was also, unfortunately, frightfully difficult to read.

Pope Benedict showed perhaps more clearly than any of his predecessors in modern times the interrelatedness of CST with the rest of Catholic doctrine. In two previous encyclicals that were not, strictly speaking, "social encyclicals" (2005's *Deus Caritas Est*, on Christian love, and 2007's *Spe Salvi*, on Christian hope), Benedict drew out strong and clear social dimensions to the doctrinal topics he addressed.

* * *

The point here is not simply to list encyclicals with the popes who wrote them and the dates of their publication. (See the chart on page 34 for that.) It's important to see that, at every step of the way, CST has grown and developed in response to the life of the society in which the Church finds itself. To be sure, CST is a body of doctrine, a set of basic moral and Christian principles. And these do not change. But it is also about applying that doctrine and those principles to the real world—to a whole range of situations and circumstances in which we live our lives together. That includes the families we're a part of, the communities we live in, the businesses and institutions where we earn our livelihood or which we own, the economy that supports those businesses and institutions, the policies and laws by which our government orders our lives.

We should also note the importance and helpfulness of the *Compendium of the Social Doctrine of the Church*. While all of the documents mentioned above were ecclesial responses to specific circumstances and situations, this compendium, published by the Pontifical Council for Justice and Peace in 2004, represents the very first attempt of the Church to offer a systematic presentation of CST.

Finally, we also have to acknowledge that bishops' conferences in some specific regions of the world have also produced pastoral letters related to CST, and some of these have been very important and influential. In particular, I'd mention the Medellin documents (1968) of the Latin American bishops conference; two documents from the United States bishops, *The Challenge of Peace* (1983) and *Economic Justice for All* (1986); and letters by bishops of more local regions, such as *This Land Is Home to Me*, a historic letter by the bishops of the Appalachian region of the United States. The fact that those documents are not mentioned prominently in this book is only because space concerns suggested I stick to documents of the universal Church.

The Major Documents
of Modern Catholic Social Teaching

1891	Leo XIII	*Rerum Novarum*	On Capital and Labor
1931	Pius XI	*Quadragesimo Anno*	On the Reconstruction of the Social Order
1961	John XXIII	*Mater et Magistra*	On Christianity and Social Progress
1963	John XXIII	*Pacem in Terris*	On Establishing Universal Peace in Truth, Justice, Charity, and Liberty
1965	Vatican II	*Gaudium et Spes*	Pastoral Constitution on the Church in the Modern World
1965	Vatican II	*Dignitatis Humanae*	Declaration on Religious Freedom
1967	Paul VI	*Populorum Progressio*	On the Development of Peoples
1971	Paul VI	*Octogesima Adveniens*	On the Occasion of the Eightieth Anniversary of the Encyclical *Rerum Novarum*
1981	John Paul II	*Laborem Exercens*	On Human Work
1981	John Paul II	*Familiaris Consortio*	On the Role of the Christian Family in the Modern World
1987	John Paul II	*Sollicitudo Rei Socialis*	On Social Concern
1991	John Paul II	*Centesimus Annus*	On the Hundredth Anniversary of *Rerum Novarum*
1995	John Paul II	*Evangelium Vitae*	On the Value and Inviolability of Human Life
2004	Pontifical Council for Justice and Peace		*Compendium of the Social Doctrine of the Church*
2009	Benedict XVI	*Caritas in Veritate*	On Integral Human Development in Charity and Truth

PART TWO

The Big Ideas

Chapter 4

Human Dignity

Tuskegee, Alabama, 1932—U.S. Public Health Service researchers initiate a study of the development and effects of syphilis in men. Six hundred men from Macon County, Georgia, are enrolled in the study, 399 of whom have syphilis.

Most of these men are local sharecroppers, black, illiterate, and living in poverty. None of them know they have syphilis going into the study, and none of them are informed of it by the researchers. "Bad blood" is what the doctors tell the men about their condition. It's a local term, and a very general one, used to refer to any number of ailments, including syphilis, anemia, and fatigue.

Originally intended to last for six months, the study is carried on for forty years. None of the men are ever treated for their illness or even warned of its nature or seriousness. Even after penicillin is introduced in 1947 and becomes widely used as an effective treatment for syphilis, the researchers do not make it available to the men or offer them the choice of quitting the study in order to be treated properly. It's only in 1972, when the Tuskegee Syphilis Study comes to light through an Associated Press newspaper report, that the whole thing is shut down.

You're bothered by this already, I know, after reading just a few paragraphs. Spend a little more time thinking about it—imagining those 399 men, their wives and the children they bore, going through day after real-life day unaware of the disease they were living with while people who could have helped them did nothing but watch and take notes—and it gets even harder to take.

"But what's the big deal?" Imagine that question for a moment, perhaps coming from a cold-hearted cynic or maybe just a friend playing devil's advocate. "It was an experiment. We do experiments like that on lab rats and monkeys all the time." Even if you're not an animal rights advocate, the question will seem obtuse at best, but probably a bit monstrous, too. Those men were not animals, you will say. They were people, human beings. And you'll point out, as if you should have to, that you can't treat people simply as specimens to be studied or tools to be used in whatever way is most convenient. (This was clear to most Americans when the study became public knowledge in 1972. The strong public outcry resulted in an immediate end to the program and several firings.) And now the topic of your conversation is—even if the phrase does not jump immediately to mind—human dignity.

Defining dignity

But what is human dignity? Where does it come from? These are harder questions than they might at first seem.

A panel of top scientists, philosophers, and scholars on the President's Council on Bioethics focused on the question just a few years ago and found themselves frustrated at the difficulty of coming up with a definition they all could agree on. One prominent member of the group, a professor of bioethics, finally dismissed human dignity as a useless concept. A Harvard psychologist published an article on the council's work that bore the provocative title "The Stupidity of Dignity."

But taking that road leads us onto very shaky ground. The men and women who produced the United Nations' Universal Declaration of Human Rights (1948), in the immediate aftermath of the devastation of World War II and the Holocaust, recognized the same challenges. Among the most eminent thinkers and leaders on the planet at the time, they acknowledged publicly that they could not reach a consensus about the origin or definition of human dignity, but still insisted in unison that it is "the foundation of freedom, justice, and peace in the world" and that it must be affirmed.

The same thinking grounds dozens of national constitutions ratified since the U.N. produced that declaration—like the Basic Law (Grundgesetz) of Germany (1949), which begins: "Human dignity is inviolable. To respect and protect it is the duty of all state authority."

And so maybe we'll have to be satisfied with the approach of the well-known American political scientist/economist Francis Fukuyama, who wrote of human dignity as a difficult-to-define "Factor X" possessed by every person that demands a fundamental level of respect that we don't owe to plants, animals, or rocks; or saying with Adam Schulman of the President's Council for Bioethics that the phrase "human dignity" serves as "a placeholder for 'whatever it is about human beings that entitles them to basic human rights and freedoms.'" (Schulman concludes, "This practice makes a good deal of sense.")

Despite the difficulty of defining it, human dignity is very real. Just about anyone who gives the matter serious consideration today will agree that we know it in our bones. It comes proclaimed clearly in the Judeo-Christian tradition, which offers us a foundational creation story in which humankind is created in the image and likeness of God. CST recognizes this as the root of all human dignity.

Because we are made in the image and likeness of God, each human person is imbued in her or his very nature with a fundamental and immeasurable value or worth to which all other persons owe a fundamental respect. This value is not earned or gained, and it's not granted by any government, circumstance, or person in authority. This value does not come as a result of some ability or skill a person has, any achievement she makes, or usefulness she has to others. It comes with being a person, pure and simple, and cannot be lost, taken away, or given up. That is human dignity.

The foundation of CST

Human dignity is at the heart of Christian morality and therefore at the heart of the entire body of modern CST. Consider:

- Pope Leo XIII pointed to human dignity in that foundational encyclical of modern CST, *Rerum Novarum*, to insist that Europe's economic life at the end of the eighteenth century was unjust and in need of change.

- Two generations later, Pope Pius XI condemned unrestrained capitalism, racism, nationalism, and totalitarianism, all for their disregard of human dignity.

- In 1961, Pope John XXIII championed human rights like no pope ever had based on convictions about human dignity.

- Human dignity was one of the fundamental ideas of the Second Vatican Council and formed its documents in some crucial ways (and even became the title of one of them: *Dignitatis Humanae*, the council's Declaration on Religious Freedom).

- Pope Paul VI insisted that human dignity be a primary consideration in all efforts toward economic and cultural development.

- Pope John Paul II made defense of human dignity a keystone of his pontificate and the basis of his defense of the rights of the poor, immigrants, the unborn, and workers, as well as the basis of his compelling criticisms of both capitalism and communism.

- Pope Benedict XVI's *Caritas in Veritate* can be read as a call for an economy and economic development programs that are attuned to, rather than fly in the face of, human dignity.

"Treat them as human beings"

One shining illustration that puts flesh on the bones of the Church's convictions about human dignity is the work of César Chávez, an important American Catholic of the twentieth century. For many today, the name is associated with a famous Mexican boxer. While I would not want to take anything from the boxer's achievements, the original César Chávez is well worth getting to know.

César began his childhood on his family's Arizona farm, but they were forced to move when the land was repossessed during the Great Depression. They joined the many thousands of migrant farm workers of the American southwest, living lives marked primarily by backbreaking work under dangerous conditions, for demeaning pay that did not begin to provide adequate food and shelter. Farm owners maintained a system that guaranteed a constant surplus of workers so that anyone who had a problem with working conditions or pay could easily be fired and replaced. Millions of American workers were protected by labor laws, but migrant workers were specifically exempted from such protections.

As a young man, César was able to escape this lifestyle and also begin to help his fellow *campesinos* as an employee of the Community Service Organization (CSO), which worked to help poor people improve their own situations and communities. César conducted voter registration drives, protested police brutality, and taught citizenship classes. By 1962, he was the CSO's general director.

But he quit his job that year, abandoning the relative comfort and security that came with it, in order to dedicate himself to building a labor union for migrant workers. César spent the rest of his life fighting, often successfully, for the rights of migrant farm workers. Through countless hours spent developing the organization and leading its members in negotiations, protests, strikes, boycotts, fasts, and other types of activism—which were often dangerous in nature—César succeeded in improving the lives of many of the poorest workers in the United States.

The motivation for this dangerous and demanding work was his intense awareness of the dignity of the *campesinos*—not a theoretical or unrealistic awareness, but a gritty and down-to-earth one. References to human dignity and its place in CST were common in César's explanations of why he did what he did when asked by reporters and admirers. He explained once:

> *In the beginning there was a lot of nonsense about the poor farm worker: "Gee, the farm worker is poor and disadvantaged and on strike, he must be a super human being!" And I said, "Cut that nonsense out, all right?" That was my opening speech: "Look, you're here working with a group of men; the farm worker is only a human being. You take the poorest of these guys and give him that ranch over there, he could be just as much of a bastard as the guy sitting there right now. Or if you think that all growers are bastards, you're no good to us either. Remember that both are men. In order to help the farm workers, look at them as human beings and not as something extra special, or else you're kidding yourself and are going to be mighty, mighty disappointed. Don't pity them either. Treat them as human beings, because they have just as many faults as you have."*

Beware the blinders

By this time, perhaps you're thinking, "OK, point well taken. Human dignity is obviously important. And unlike the ivory tower academic who wrote about 'the stupidity of dignity,' I get it. I do recognize and respect human dignity in my daily life. I'd have wanted nothing to do with the Tuskegee syphilis experiment. No need to belabor the point further."

For most of us, in other words, it all really does seem rather obvious. Or does it?

One fact we must contend with is the moral blinders that we too often tend to wear when it comes to some circumstances or situations in which human dignity is called into question. Unfortunately, it is sometimes unclear to well-intentioned and reasonable people what exactly the demands of human dignity include.

The immorality of slavery seems obvious today. And yet in the early nineteenth century, thousands of good American people owned slaves. Most Catholics and their leaders accepted it and even defended it as morally acceptable. One of the most influential moral theology textbooks of the time said that neither the natural law nor the Bible forbids slavery, and before 1861, not a single American bishop objected to it. Indeed, a century later, the Catholic contribution to the historic civil rights movement was minimal.

Those growers that César Chávez opposed—the ones who paid so little, provided miserable working conditions to their employees, and ignored pleas for things as simple as time for a water break or a place to go to the bathroom out in the fields—they were not evil people. Indeed, many were churchgoing Catholics themselves.

I was stunned and depressed recently, as I read an article about the 1994 genocide in Rwanda, to learn that many Catholics, indeed many priests and nuns, were active participants in the slaughter. That event was surely one of the most egregious examples of the trampling of human dignity in living memory.

History teaches us all too clearly that it's easy for certain images of what it means to be a person to form the unconscious lens through which we see ourselves and others. We end up, perhaps innocently, presuming some types of persons (those like us) or cultures (those like our own) to be superior to others. My culture not only appears natural, but it appears to be nature itself. When we do this, we're making God in our own image. Theologian Virgilio Elizondo writes that when people are rejected by those around them because of personal characteristics like skin color or way of life, the experience "brands the soul, in a way worse and more permanent than a branding of the master's mark with a hot iron on the face."

And so I must search my conscience, my heart, my attitudes and choices. What are my own personal blinders preventing me from seeing? What blinders do I perhaps share with those around me in my immediate community, family, social class, or country? What are my attitudes toward unborn people? People who have immigrated from poorer nations? People who are gay?

It is only by asking these uncomfortable questions that we can be sure to avoid disregarding the dignity, branding the soul, of one who is made in the image of God.

Chapter 5

Solidarity

Like a bicycle that goes nowhere without two good wheels, Catholic Social Teaching has two central ideas on which everything else balances and rides along. One wheel is human dignity, the subject of chapter 4. The second wheel, solidarity, is just as essential to what CST is all about.

Interdependence

Our human and global interdependence is a fact—as true and unavoidable as the bellybuttons we all bear on our bodies—and it seems to become truer with each passing year. We are all related, our lives interconnected with one another. That's most obvious in terms of my immediate family, as those aforementioned bellybuttons attest! My navel is, of course, literally a scar on my skin that reminds me of the physical connectedness I once had with my mother, fully dependent on her for the life I had, the life-sustaining nourishment I received, and the earliest development I went through. (Thanks, Mom!)

A test of the blood coursing through my veins will confirm pretty quickly that more than one person is responsible for my being here. My dad is part of me, too. Consider genetics a little longer and it soon becomes clear that even more people had a role in the fact that I exist and who I am.

Though this interdependence is clear with my family, it's not limited to them. In ways that are literally innumerable, I'm dependent upon and connected at this moment with people around the planet: the farmers who grew the wheat and sugar in the cereal I just had for breakfast, the miners who dug the coal that makes the electricity that powers the computer in front of me now, the teachers who taught me as a child how to spell and write, the people around the planet who can buy this book on a variety of Internet websites long after my work on it is complete.

All of this interconnectedness can be good (think about the explosion of information available to people almost everywhere or the massive U.S. aid to help fight AIDS in Africa); but it can also be dangerous (consider the wrecking of the world's environment or global terrorism).

Solidarity

Interdependence is a fact. The moral response to that fact is solidarity. Solidarity is an awareness of the unity of the human family, the oneness that I share with every other person. It is, in Pope Benedict XVI's words, "a recognition that the human race is a single family working together in true communion, not simply a group of subjects who happen to live side by side." Before I am a citizen of a particular country or a member of a particular race, I am a human person and a member of the human family.

Solidarity is not just about knowing all this; it's about acting on it. While global interdependence has the potential to threaten the common good, as I noted above, solidarity is the determination to act in such a way that it will bring good to the human community.

Pope John Paul II offered what has become the classic description of solidarity in CST in his 1987 encyclical *Sollicitudo Rei Socialis.* Solidarity, he wrote,

> is not a feeling of vague compassion or shallow distress at the misfortunes of so many people, both near and far. On the contrary, it is a firm and persevering determination to commit oneself to the common good; that is to say to the good of all and of each individual, because we are all really responsible for all.

> Solidarity helps us to see the "other"—whether a person, people or nation—not just as some kind of instrument, with a work capacity and physical strength to be exploited at low cost and then discarded when no longer useful, but as our "neighbor," a "helper" (see Genesis 2:18–20), to be made a sharer, on a par with ourselves, in the banquet of life to which all are equally invited by God. Hence the importance of reawakening the religious awareness

of individuals and peoples. Thus the exploitation, oppression and annihilation of others are excluded.

For example, one hero of solidarity that Pope John Paul II pointed to in the same encyclical is Saint Peter Claver, a seventeenth-century Spanish priest. In Colombia, a colony of Spain, Claver ministered selflessly to the men and women who were sold as slaves in "the new world." He is perhaps best known for hurrying to the port of Cartegna whenever he saw a slave ship pulling into dock. Without waiting for the miserable human cargo to be unloaded at the end of a god-awful voyage, he boarded the ship, entered the stinking and fetid hull where the slaves were stored, and began offering whatever aid and comfort he could. Peter did not simply see the circumstances and wish it weren't so, and he was not content with prayers or letters to people of influence. He made himself a companion to those who were suffering. That is solidarity.

"This is the plan that revolves around you"

Solidarity can be a real challenge for us Americans. American culture encourages us to embrace and celebrate individualism and self-sufficiency. We admire those who can survive and thrive on their own, with the help of no one. We have what theologian Maureen H. O'Connell calls a "preoccupation with remaining physically, emotionally, financially, and nationally invulnerable." We even create fictional heroes who embody that: the Lone Ranger, Batman, Wolverine.

On the positive side, these ideals push us to be resilient, creative, and strong individuals. That's not something to minimize. But there are other ideals that "made America what it is" and allowed our nation to enjoy the successes that it has. Promoters of rugged individualism leave out some other important characteristics, and we do that to our peril.

Where self-sufficiency is the paramount virtue:

- community is deemed unnecessary.
- interdependence is considered dangerous.
- poverty or other kinds of need are resented, distrusted, and seen as personal failure.
- wealth and success are seen as purely personal achievement.

These statements reflect a distorted view of reality. They are also corrosive of a strong commitment to living the virtue of solidarity. We are raised, for example, to see climbing the economic and social ladder as an important sign of success and strength. We strive to remove ourselves as far as we can, even geographically, from poverty and adversity. But solidarity calls us closer to it. In living solidarity, we move closer to suffering not for the sake of suffering, but out of a desire to be near to those who are unable to escape it, to accompany them in it, and perhaps to bring some relief to the suffering, even if it's only by our presence. (Note that the root of the English word *compassion* means "suffering with.")

Furthermore, let's not discount the even more obvious impact of human weakness on the virtue of solidarity. By human weakness, individualism is also expressed as selfishness and self-centeredness. We see it expressed in the widespread ads for a cell phone plan in which we're told "this is the plan that revolves around you" (as we watch an array of exciting devices literally revolve in mid-air around certain consumers). This seemingly benevolent commercial expresses some discouraging things about American culture.

The God in whose image we're made

The Catholic moral vision, on the other hand, proposes something very different. As we emphasized in the last chapter, on human dignity, each person is created in the image of God. But it is crucial to remember who this God, in whose image we are created, is.

God does not exist in eternal solitary oneness. God's very self is a communion of persons, Father, Son, and Holy Spirit. As theologian David Hollenbach writes, "the One God is not an isolated monad but rather three persons in relationships of absolute self-communication and communion. The self-communication in love by the three divine persons is so total that God is radically one." This is the remarkable understanding of God, revealed to us by him, that allowed the Apostle John to assert not just that God loves or that God is loving, but that God is love.

Consider then what it means to be made in the image of God! To be a person is, by definition, to be in relation to others. While every individual person is made in the image of God, there is something about human society itself that is also an image of God.

It is beautifully fitting and consistent, then, that God's plan of salvation for humanity was a revelation of incredible solidarity. In the Incarnation of God, God became one with us. The Son of God "emptied himself" (Philippians 2:6) to take on human form. And so the *Compendium of the Social Doctrine of the Church* calls Jesus the "unsurpassed apex" of solidarity.

The more we consider it, the more we see that the Catholic vision of humanity is shot through with relationality: the Trinity, God, and humanity, the Church as the body of Christ, the communion of saints, the collegiality of bishops, local churches and church universal, and on we could go.

And so, while the virtue of solidarity is surely not a uniquely Christian ideal—it does not take faith to understand it, and there are plenty of non-Christians, even atheists, who live it far more authentically, even heroically, than many Catholics—Christian faith does deepen our understanding of it, shed some light on the source and meaning of it, and certainly provides added motivation for embracing it as a style of living.

Dorothy Day

One hero of human solidarity was the twentieth-century American woman Dorothy Day (1897–1980). In her early-adult years, Dorothy worked as a journalist and hung out among the Bohemian writers and artists of Greenwich Village, living a life that included sexual promiscuity, an abortion, and a divorce. Even then, she had a strong inclination toward human solidarity, especially toward the poor and the weak, which drew her interest toward anarchism, socialism, and the women's suffrage movement. A religious conversion changed her personal life in dramatic ways, but only deepened her awareness of the bonds she shared with all people, especially the weakest around her.

With French immigrant Peter Maurin, she founded the Catholic Worker movement in New York in 1933. In the midst of the Depression, they opened a house of hospitality in New York City, where the poor could find meals, a place to sleep, and acceptance. Soon there were Catholic Worker houses around New York City and then the country. Dorothy and Peter's newspaper, *The Catholic Worker*, gained a wide, national readership.

Dorothy insisted on the importance of voluntary poverty—not only helping the poor, but living among them as one of them. Her personal diaries reveal that it was rarely an easy way of living. She wrote about life in community as "this awful intimacy" and "surely like a cross." One journal entry from 1958 notes, "While meeting goes on Larry is drunk in office. Ellen fighting in hall, Dan and Ramon shouting in hall. Anna sweeping the hall. Friday nights are getting to be hell."

And yet she lived this life until her death in 1980. Indeed, part of the greatness of Dorothy Day is that—as Robert Ellsberg has put it— "there was absolutely no distinction between what she believed, what she wrote, and the manner in which she lived."

Solidarity in our own lives

Dorothy's witness compels me to ask myself: What about the way I live? What about the way we live our lives together?

Because our lifestyles are so individualized today, the first steps in a lifestyle of deeper solidarity can be simple and inviting. We can begin spending more time among those who are too often ignored or forgotten in our own families or towns: the elderly, the sick, the unacceptably different. We can shop at farmers markets and volunteer with community organizations.

Solidarity is not just about giving money where it's needed. It's also about physical presence, friendship, accompaniment, and moral imagination. It's a refusal to abide the walls that society constructs between people of different classes. Solidarity could mean getting to know the person who fixes my car or cleans my office.

We can also begin to expand our view, asking how well we've been living like we truly are one with those outside our most immediate communities, outside our social class, outside our own race or gender. We might consider purchasing fair trade products, which are produced through a system that avoids the exploitation of poor farmers in impoverished regions. We might also ask if our political convictions express an appreciation of solidarity.

We have covered the two primary concepts of CST: human dignity and human solidarity. All the rest flows from taking these two ideas seriously.

Chapter 6

Human Rights

It's one thing to say I love my car or that my car is important to me. But if I never change the oil, how much do I really love my car? The car's manual provides a list of ways to treat my car well, and common sense provides plenty more. Changing the oil, rotating the tires, and avoiding demolition derbies are all ways that I put respect for the vehicle into action. They make it real. Ignoring them means I end up with a car that I may say I love, but which I've turned into junk.

What oil changes are to car-loving, human rights are to human dignity and solidarity. They make human dignity and solidarity concrete, bring them into the real world, make them part of our laws, our culture, our daily lives. Human rights give teeth to human dignity and solidarity. When we ignore human rights, any talk of human dignity or solidarity is either empty banter, embarrassing hypocrisy, or exploitive lies.

What are human rights?

Rights are ethical norms that must be honored and conditions that must exist to ensure the well-being of persons. Some rights aren't human rights. If you're an adult American citizen who has never been convicted of a felony, you have a right to vote in our elections; not everyone can do that. If you're an employer, you have a right, under certain conditions, to fire your employees; not everyone can do that, either.

But human rights are dependent on nothing—not accomplishments or economic status, not religious beliefs or personal goodness, not presence within the borders of some nation or agreement with some government policy—nothing but being a human person. The thirteenth amendment to the U.S. Constitution, which outlawed slavery, did not give black people in America the right to be free. It recognized a right that they already possessed, but which laws in the United States had, until then, failed to recognize.

Catholics can be proud that their Church has stood in recent decades at the forefront of the effort to recognize and protect human rights throughout the world. In 1963, Pope John XXIII provided powerful momentum for Catholic involvement in the global human rights movement. More recently, Pope John Paul II strode the world stage for more than a quarter-century as one of the world's most respected and influential defenders of human rights.

And it's not just about popes. Nourished by their faith and the convictions about human dignity instilled in them by CST, individual Catholics have, in the past half-century, acted as powerful leaders in the midst of dramatic and dangerous struggles for human rights in Poland, El Salvador, the Philippines, East Timor, South Africa, and elsewhere.

It wasn't always so

But it was not always this way. Human rights thinking as we know it today had its start "outside the Church," in England at the end of the 1600s. It grew out of the Enlightenment, which represented a rejection of much of the Church's authority and doctrines. But "outside the Church" is relative.

In 1689, the Parliament of England produced the English Bill of Rights, a historic statement of the basic rights of all English people. To be sure, it was no Church document. But British history and culture had been nourished and driven by Christianity for a thousand years prior. Even though the Enlightenment surely was a rejection of some of that ancient patrimony, and many Church leaders at the time perceived Enlightenment thinking as a threat, it is surely unrealistic and unfair to suggest that the Christian worldview had nothing to do with the new Bill of Rights.

Human rights thinking came out in force a century later, first with the American Revolution, and even more dramatically (and in many ways tragically) in the French Revolution that immediately followed. The American Declaration of Independence (1776) makes clear that human rights had a central place in the vision of America's founders. It speaks of certain "truths" that they took to be "self-evident" (that is, so obvious in human experience and human nature as to need no proof): "that all men are created equal, that they are endowed by their Creator with certain unalienable Rights, that among these are Life, Liberty and the pursuit of Happiness."

A little more than a decade later, the Bill of Rights of the U.S. Constitution went further in identifying such rights, acknowledging freedom of religion, speech, and assembly, among others. It became a landmark statement of the place of human rights in modern democracies. In 1789, in the midst of the French Revolution, the French Assembly produced the Declaration of the Rights of Man, a similar summary of human rights.

Looking back today, we can see this broad new recognition of every person's most fundamental rights as a significant step in the moral development of Western society. But Church leaders did not see it this way at the time. That's because many other new ideas, ones that truly were threatening to the existence of the Church, came along with it, and also because, in the case of France, the convictions were forced into society and government with a violent disregard for anything that stood in their way—including, in some cases, human rights!

It's easy to say in hindsight that the Church could have been more careful about distinguishing between the good and the bad elements of the French Revolution. But in "the fog of war" (and a war against the Church is, in some ways, what the French Revolution was), such distinctions can be difficult to make.

And so in 1791, Pope Pius VI condemned the French Assembly's Declaration of the Rights of Man, opposing the Church not only to the revolution's rejection of its authority to teach in the name of God, but also to ideas like freedom of religion and freedom of the press. Unfortunately, this stance set in and became the Church's attitude toward everything associated in any way with modern thinking about individual autonomy and rights. In an 1832 encyclical, Pope Gregory XVI flatly condemned, without nuance, freedom of conscience, freedom of opinion, and free speech as "absurd and erroneous." A generation later, Pope Pius IX listed freedom of religion and freedom of worship among the pernicious errors of the day.

Some suggest that's where things stood until Pope John and Vatican II came along. But that version fails to notice the Church's earlier promotion of some important human rights at a time when most of Western society was turning a blind eye to them. We've already spoken of Pope Leo XIII's *Rerum Novarum* (1891) and Pope Pius XI's *Quadragesimo Anno* (1931), which championed the rights of workers to organize, strike, receive a just wage, and own property. A decade after the latter document, Pope Pius XII used a 1941 radio address to call for the formulation of an international bill of rights founded on the dignity of the human person.

During those decades, this rights thinking developing within the Church influenced Catholic figures in the Christian Democrat and Christian Socialist parties of some European and Latin American nations. As a result, it soon found a place in the constitutions of some of these nations. Government representatives of these same nations had an important part in the decision of the United Nations to take up, in 1945, the task of developing the sort of statement Pius XII had called for just four years earlier.

One influential and trusted voice among the thinkers and leaders who played a part in the preparation of that statement was Jacques Maritain, a prominent philosopher of the day. Maritain's thinking was rooted deep in his Catholic faith, and for him, the social encyclicals of Leo XIII and Pius XI held an important place in that.

In 1948, the United Nations ratified the Universal Declaration of Human Rights. This historic document included many rights of a political and civil nature that had been included in the French Declaration of the Rights of Man and the American Bill of Rights long before. But it marked what noted human rights scholar Aryeh Neier calls "a radical break with its predecessors" by also insisting on many economic and social rights—that is, the very rights that Popes Leo XIII and Pius XI had advocated several decades earlier. In short, the Universal Declaration of Human Rights and the long cultural development that preceded it has strong (though sometimes hidden) Catholic roots.

The U.N. Declaration has been the most important reference point for discussion and policy on human rights ever since. It has led to other important institutions, including the International Criminal Tribunals that prosecuted those who committed grave crimes against humanity in Yugoslavia and Rwanda; the U.S. State Department's Bureau of Democracy, Human Rights, and Labor; and effective nongovernmental organizations like Amnesty International and Human Rights Watch.

A new era in Catholic human rights thinking

After World War II, the Cold War between the United States (and its Western allies) and the Soviet Union raged, and at its height, in October 1962, the Cuban Missile Crisis suddenly held the world in fear of nuclear calamity for several days. As American and Soviet warships faced off in the Atlantic Ocean, each awaiting orders from above, a critical intervention from Pope John XXIII directly to the two nations' leaders provided an opportunity for Soviet Premier Nikita Khrushchev to turn his ships around in a way that framed the move as a moment of peace-seeking rather than backing down. As a result, the Pope emerged as one of the heroes of that crisis.

With the world both acutely aware of the disaster that it had narrowly averted and especially willing to hear what the Pope might have to say, John, who already knew at the time that he was dying of cancer (though it was not public knowledge), decided the moment was right to make a bold statement about world peace. On April 11, 1963, six months after the Cuban Missile Crisis and less than two months before he would die, he released *Pacem in Terris* ("Peace on Earth").

The document was not what you might expect, given its title. At face value anyway, it wasn't a call for stronger efforts at peacemaking or a stern rebuke to proponents of the arms race. For his historic world peace encyclical, Good Pope John chose to address human rights. In fact, he offered a thorough, powerful, and persuasive statement on human rights to which no other pope or bishop of the Church has come close in the half-century since.

Pope John provides a summary of human rights, mostly found in sections 11 to 27 of *Pacem in Terris.* They include rights to:

life	freedom of worship
bodily integrity	freedom to choose one's state of life
food	freedom to form a family
clothing	freedom of initiative in business
shelter	work
rest	adequate working conditions
medical care	proper wage
necessary social services	private property
respect for one's person	productive goods
a good reputation	freedom of assembly and association
freedom to search for truth	freedom of movement and residence
freedom of speech	emigrate and immigrate
freedom of information	active participation in public affairs
education	share in the benefits of culture
juridical protection of rights	act freely and responsibly

Pope John pointed out three essential aspects of these rights. All human rights are:

universal: that is, all people have them, simply by being people, no matter who they are;

inviolable: no person, group, or government may violate them, no matter who they are;

unalienable: no person can ever lose or surrender his or her own human rights, no matter the circumstances.

Pope John Paul II would later add a fourth characteristic to the list. They are also *indivisible:* no person or government can pick and choose which of them are to be recognized, as though shopping at a grocery store deli.

While Western ideas about human rights often amount to protecting individuals from the people who surround them, Pope John's vision of human rights—the Catholic Church's vision—is about the rights of a person in community. In this vision, the dignity of each person is most protected and can flourish best in a community where all flourish together. Human rights are about the minimum conditions necessary for individual flourishing, but they are also about the minimum conditions necessary for a flourishing community life. The rights that I have and that others must respect are balanced with the duties that I have to the others around me and to the community (local, global, national) within which I live.

In other words, while it is certainly true that human rights flow directly from the idea of human dignity, it is also true that they flow directly from the idea of solidarity. That's why John XXIII could so comfortably connect peace in the world with human rights.

Threats to human rights today

Human rights remain a major issue in places throughout the world today. Current issues include:

- the arrest and detention of prominent bloggers in **Vietnam** for the expression of political opinions critical of the nation's government;

- the incarceration of political prisoners in **Burma**;

- the imprisonment of girls and women in **Afghanistan** for "running away" from home;

- the torture and execution of detainees in the armed conflict in **Syria**;

- the torture and disappearance of human rights activists in **United Arab Emirates**.

In a June 2012 op-ed in *The New York Times*, former U.S. President Jimmy Carter pointed out that the **United States** has some important human rights issues of its own that demand attention and reform. These include the indefinite detention of suspected terrorists, drone strikes, and torture.

CST provides all the motivation any Catholic needs to become involved in any of these issues, at levels high and low, in order to help find solutions.

Chapter 7

The Common Good

I f the common good were a person rather than an idea, I'd be tempted to feel sorry for the poor guy saddled with such a humdrum name. Especially when he's standing alongside his friends, with jazzy names like universal destination of goods, solidarity, and preferential option for the poor. It's like putting a guy named John Smith in a room with Hulk Hogan, Shaquille O'Neal, and Lady Gaga.

Oh, but get to know him and see him in action, this guy with the plain-Jane name, and I'd no longer feel sorry for him, and I certainly would not be bored. I'd be inspired, challenged, and a bit intimidated. If the common good were a person, he would be one of the most striking people we've ever met, remarkable for his steely compassion and unflinching generosity.

Along with human rights, the common good gives teeth to the dual principles of human dignity and solidarity. We can talk very abstractly and theoretically about human dignity and solidarity; but living them out, weaving them into our personal lives, social lives, family lives, and political lives means respecting human rights and promoting the common good.

The common good is the social context of human dignity. It is the social support of human rights. In order for the common good to be a viable, relevant concept, we have to recognize ourselves as members of a society together—that is, we have to embrace solidarity.

What is the common good?

Most of us have a very real and vivid experience of the common good lived on a small scale in family life. In a healthy family, the well-being of all those who make it up are tightly, intentionally, and unavoidably bound together—so much so that each member regards every other member's well-being as his or her own. What hurts my wife, daughter, son, or parent hurts me. What is good for any of them is good for me. If my wife is gravely ill or my child is in serious trouble, there's no way I can simply go happily on with my own life, attending to my own concerns, offering a quick "good luck with that problem" before I head out the door each day to go about my business. Their pain distresses me, but it also negatively impacts my own life, the lives of my kids, and the smooth functioning of our household. Furthermore, I know in my bones that I'm morally accountable for how my attitudes and actions affect my family. I have a responsibility to do things that will build up my family's well-being and avoid things that will harm that well-being.

Understand that and you understand the idea of the common good. But the common good expands that vision to a wider field. It asks me to realize that the concerns of a broader society—our community, our nation, even our world—are my concerns, too. I am accountable not only for how my actions affect my family and me, but for how they affect society and everyone it. My well-being is inescapably tied to the well-being of the society around me. We are all in this together.

Before the 1960s, the common good was generally understood in Catholic teaching to mean seeking the good of the region, empire, or nation in which one lived. As modern life made us all interdependent on a global scale, the Second Vatican Council expanded that understanding to include all people of the world:

> *Every day human interdependence grows more tightly drawn and spreads by degrees over the whole world. As a result the common good, that is, the sum of those conditions of social life which allow social groups and their individual members relatively thorough and ready access to their own fulfillment, today takes on an increasingly universal complexion and consequently involves rights and duties with respect to the whole human race. Every social group must take account of the needs and legitimate aspirations of other groups, and even of the general welfare of the entire human family.*

Never against individual goods

The family analogy brings out an important aspect of the common good that is often misunderstood. Consider: My wife and I cannot decide that in order for us to afford the newer car our family will be needing soon, each of the kids will take his or her turn not eating for a week at a time, thus saving on groceries. We don't secure our family's well-being at the expense of the needs and development of any individual person in it. In fact, just the opposite is usually the case. We improve our family's well-being by making sure every individual gets things they deserve and need. Family life lived well makes each of us much better, and able to succeed much more readily, than we ever could have been or done if left to ourselves.

Society works the same way. The common good and each person's individual good are not opposites, and they are not contrary to one another. They're interlocked. They are dimensions of each other. The common good includes the good of individuals and also the good of families and all other groups. The common good is the good of one and all. It's about using our talents and using our personal autonomy, but it's also about cooperating with others and building up the community.

Take away concern for either the common good or individual rights in a society and the other collapses quickly, too. Pope John Paul II was strident in his insistence on this idea. For example, he notes that it's impossible to promote the common good and disregard an individual's right to life.

And so speaking of the common good is not code for socialism, if by socialism you mean Marxist totalitarianism. It does not mean that basic individual goods must be sacrificed, whatever the cost, in the name of the good of the group. The common good, as Catholic Social Teaching understands it, affirms individuals, their rights, and their liberties.

But it's never only about me

However, there's more to it. Last night my wife (the primary bill-payer in our family) said to me, "With this week's mortgage payment, plus Nick's first Communion gift and cake, plus Gianna's field trip on

Wednesday, we'll be a little tight on funds around here until next payday." Understood. That's my wife's way of saying, "Don't go buying any books this week."

Do I have a right to buy a book with my hard-earned money? You're darn right I do, and I know my wife agrees. But there are times when doing without the book, even one I really want, is not only the kind thing to do, but what I need to do for the common good of my family.

As morally responsible persons, we can't be satisfied simply with acting out of self-interest. Society is not a free play area where individuals pursue whatever goods they can get for themselves. When people are simply left to fend for themselves, the human dignity of all suffers. Isn't it clear by now that an every-man-for-himself mentality has dragged down our culture, and each of us with it, in innumerable ways? Me-first morality—whether we're talking about sexual ethics, business ethics, or economic ethics—hurts people, is contrary to human dignity, and flies in the face of Catholic Social Teaching.

The common good is my good

Besides, even if I were inclined to attempt to look at life from a purely individualistic point of view, ignoring the common good would still be dumb, because it works against my own self-interest anyway. There are goods that cannot be achieved privately; we must live in a well-functioning society to realize them. No, that's not saying enough. In fact, there are no goods that can truly be achieved privately. If that's true on a spiritual level (and the Catholic faith is adamant that it is, on many levels), it is no less true on a temporal level.

"Hey, I make my own success," I'm tempted to object. "I earn my own paycheck through my own hard work. Nobody hands me anything." And there's no question in my own mind that I do earn it. Without the daily hard work (which I do at a Catholic publishing company), not to mention the years of work that got me here, I'd quickly fail. But just a few moments of consideration will make clear that I'm the only one in the frame of that picture because I'm the one drawing the frame, and I've drawn it quite narrowly, like cropping out the folks around me in a digital image. I have this job that gets me that paycheck for a thousand reasons beyond my own hard work. The first ten that come to mind are:

1. From the moment of my conception, by God's grace and my parents' genetic makeup, I was handed a certain set of abilities, skills, and predispositions that made me able to do and enjoy this job.

2. My mother loved me enough not to abort me (and if she had been so inclined, the law at the time helped protect me from that fate).

3. My parents were attentive to my healthy early development —physically, intellectually, emotionally, socially—throughout my childhood.

4. My dad offered a great example of a husband and father who responsibly works hard at a job day in and day out to support his family.

5. A teacher taught me to read. (Her paycheck, by the way, came from local tax dollars.)

6. Other teachers developed the innumerable mental and intellectual skills I use daily. (More paychecks from more tax dollars, until I was off to college, an experience funded by my parents, my diocese, and the federal government.)

7. I can drive to work on roads that were and continue to be paid for by tax revenue of people throughout my state.

8. A bunch of other talented people come to work every day at the same place and do their jobs very well.

9. All the people who buy the books we publish also had teachers who taught them to read years ago. And those people can afford to buy the books because they earn their own paychecks, thanks in part to their own parents and their own good teachers.

10. Local, state, and federal law enforcement maintains an orderly society around me in which all of the above can happen.

It is not one or the other—my own hard work is essential to my own success, but so is a host of other people and groups and circumstances.

I am crazy and insufferably self-centered to think I somehow earned my good life on my own (and by the same token just as unrealistic to think that each person who is poor is solely responsible for his own poverty).

When we ignore all of that, and fail to work for the common good, we opt instead for a common bad, a society that does not support what I need to live a good life. We are each dependent on each other for material and economic well-being, our cultural and spiritual well-being. We are interdependent. We share each other's fate.

Difficult business

One area of life all of this relates to in a special way is politics, since promotion of the common good is the very reason for the existence of government. (More on this in chapter 14.) But it would be a mistake to think that unless I'm a politician, I'm exempt from having to bother myself with concerns about the common good, or that I only need consider these concerns on election day. Every person and group within society is called to pursue the common good, each in our own ways. "To desire the common good and strive towards it," writes Pope Benedict in *Caritas in Veritate*, the most recent social encyclical, "is a requirement of justice and charity."

In fact, if it's only politicians who are working at it while the rest of us are going about our looking-out-for-number-one lives, laws and policies won't be worth much at all. Pope Paul VI pulled no punches on this point:

> *Legislation is necessary, but it is not sufficient for setting up true relationships of justice and equity. In teaching us charity, the Gospel instructs us in the preferential respect due to the poor and the special situation they have in society: the more fortunate should renounce some of their rights so as to place their goods more generously at the service of others. If, beyond legal rules, there is really no deeper feeling of respect for and service to others, then even equality before the law can serve as an alibi for flagrant discrimination, continued exploitation and actual contempt. Without a renewed education in solidarity, an overemphasis of equality can give rise to an individualism in which each one claims his own rights without wishing to be answerable for the common good.*

This is difficult business. The common good is not calculus. There is no set of equations to which we turn which make obvious in every situation and circumstance just what the common good demands. Seeking the common good means making prudential judgments—honestly and unflinchingly, without trying to fool others or even ourselves. What choice, what action, what policy will best promote the good health of the community (local/national/global) and all those who make it up? It takes courage, commitment, and selflessness to follow through on those prudential judgments, along with the humility to recognize in discussions with others that prudential judgments are what they are.

It means, for example, that asking myself, "Are you better off today than you were four years ago?" might not be the most relevant question to answer in making a choice about how to cast a vote. It means deciding what job is going to get me the highest income might not be the most crucial factor in choosing a career path. It means identifying which course of action is going to make me feel most fulfilled, or having the most personal satisfaction (or fun) might not be the best question to ask when deciding how to deal with a shaky marriage.

And the virtues it takes to do these things do not come easily to us today. Theologian Maureen H. O'Connell puts it well:

> Generally speaking, our hyper-individualized, privatized, and commercialized climate in contemporary American culture calls into question whether any kind of collective commitment to life in community is possible. We simply are not concerned with the public or common good, and even in the moments when we are so concerned, we have failed to habituate the public virtues that translate that concern into collective action.

Feeling a little sting with one or more of those observations? I hope so—I'd hate to be alone in confronting the uncomfortable demands, and working through occasional personal failures, when it comes to being attentive to the common good.

Chapter 8

The Universal Destination of Goods

Catholic leaders, in the Church and in public life, occasionally get themselves into trouble by "taking too seriously" Catholic moral teaching. Politicians are accused of trying to impose their religion through policies and laws. Bishops are accused of meddling in the most private aspects of people's lives. Usually these controversies are related to Church teaching on sexuality, marriage, and respect for human life.

But if you think folks scream, "Stay out of my private life!" at the mention of these topics, just wait until word gets out—and it hasn't—that the Church's understanding of what it really means to own something is different than what most Americans mean, and that the Church has something to say about what each of us morally can and can't do with what we own. Politicians, beware: Now we're talking about becoming truly unelectable!

I'm referring to Church teaching on the universal destination of goods (or, put a little more clearly, the social purpose of private property). And make no mistake, it's an idea that pope after pope has insisted must have a place in our public life. John Paul II called it "the first principle of the whole ethical and social order" and "the characteristic principle of Christian social doctrine."

Let's be clear from the start: The Church supports our right to own private property. In *Rerum Novarum*, the foundational document of modern Catholic Social Teaching, Pope Leo XIII argued that this right is found in natural law. Human beings, he pointed out, need private property to live a decent life, a life of dignity. We have to provide for ourselves and our families, and to do this effectively, he said, we need to be able to own stuff, to possess things in a stable and permanent way. Leo cited the Tenth Commandment and the great theologian Saint Thomas Aquinas in support of his point.

Not an 'untouchable' right

So far, so good, right? After all, it would never occur to most of us in the West even to look for philosophical and scriptural support for it; we consider our right to property to be obvious, self-evident. And yet, despite the Pope's conviction that this right must be defended, Leo went on to provide some important nuances to the teaching. He said that it's one thing to have a right to possess things, but entirely another to think we have a right to do whatever we want with what we own.

Huh? But isn't that what owning something means? It's mine to do with whatever I want, right? Nope, says the Pope. He writes that we have a duty to provide help to those who are poor, quoting Thomas Aquinas (whose words he earlier used to support his argument for private property): "Man should not consider his material possessions as his own, but as common to all, so as to share them without hesitation when others are in need."

As clear as Leo is on this, he placed far more emphasis on the right to private property than on relative nature of this right. In fact, compared to what was to come in subsequent Church teaching, Leo comes off sounding almost halfhearted about it.

Popes Pius XI, Pius XII, John XXIII, Paul VI, John Paul II, and Benedict XVI—as well as the Second Vatican Council, the *Catechism of the Catholic Church*, and the *Compendium of the Social Doctrine of the Church*—all have been clear and emphatic: "Christian tradition has never upheld this right [to private property] as absolute and untouchable. On the contrary, it has always understood this right within the broader context of the right common to all to use the goods of the whole of creation: the right to private property is subordinated to the right to common use, to the fact that goods are meant for everyone." (That's how John Paul II put it in his 1981 encyclical, *Laborem Exercens*.)

In short, when the right to private property comes in conflict with the common good, the common good always trumps private property. (Interestingly, John Paul II developed CST by including not just physical goods—the food, land, and fuels that have been important to survival for centuries—among "the goods of the earth" to which all people have some right, but also valuable intangibles like education, understanding, skills, and access to technology.) A hard teaching, to be sure. But don't blame these modern popes. They didn't make it up. The idea has strong roots in the Bible and Christian tradition.

In the Old Testament, God demanded of the Israelites that farmers leave some food in their fields at harvest time so that the poor may have access to it, that they cancel debts owed to them by the poor every seven years, and that every fifty years ancestral lands that had been lost through debt or poverty be restored to the original owners (Leviticus 19:9–10; Deuteronomy 24:19–21; Deuteronomy 15:1–2; Leviticus 25). In the New Testament, Jesus—known for his compassion and willingness to forgive—tells the story of the rich man who went to hell because he didn't share his food with a poor man outside his door (Luke 16:19–31).

What did the early Christian community make of this? "The community of believers was of one heart and mind, and no one claimed that any of his possessions was his own, but they had everything in common....There was no needy person among them, for those who owned property or houses would sell them, bring the proceeds of the sale, and put them at the feet of the apostles, and they were distributed to each according to need" (Acts 4:32–35; see also Acts 2:43–47).

The Fathers of the Church, early Christianity's greatest theologians and interpreters of Scripture, recognized this social purpose of private property clearly in the Bible, and they expected Christians to live it. The great fourth-century bishop, Saint Ambrose of Milan, wrote, "When giving to the poor you are not giving him what is yours; rather you are paying back to him what is his. Indeed what is common to all and has been given to all to make use of, you have usurped for yourself alone." The same idea is also found in the writings and homilies of Saints Clement of Alexandria, Gregory of Nazianzus, and John Chrysostom.

Medieval theologian Thomas Aquinas, mentioned already, taught that private property is a reasonable thing, but that a person in extreme necessity can legitimately take what he needs from someone else, and it's not stealing, not a sin, because in situations of dire need, all things are common.

Real-world consequences

Clearly, in presenting the social purpose of private property to Catholics today, the popes are only being faithful to the truths that have been handed on to us. The social purpose of private property is a logical conclusion to what we have already said about solidarity and the common good. Solidarity, after all, says we are one human family, and the common good insists we treat each other like family, treating one another's good as if it were our own good. I don't know about your family life, but in our house growing up, private property was never absolute, and sharing was never optional. (It's not surprising, then, that the compilers of the *Compendium of the Social Teaching of the Church* placed the section on the universal destination of goods immediately after the one on the common good, saying that the universal destination of goods is "[a]mong the numerous implications of the common good.") We said earlier that the common good is one of the principles (along with human rights) that gives teeth to human dignity and solidarity. Sometimes those teeth have some bite to them!

For example, in 1965, the bishops of the world, in *Gaudium et Spes*, one of the most important documents of Vatican II, pointed out the vast rural estates of South America "which are only slightly cultivated or lie completely idle for the sake of profit, while the majority of the people either are without land or have only very small fields, and, on the other hand, it is evidently urgent to increase the productivity of the fields." The council document called for land reform:

> that income may grow, working conditions should be improved, security in employment increased, and an incentive to working on one's own initiative given. Indeed, insufficiently cultivated estates should be distributed to those who can make these lands fruitful; in this case, the necessary things and means, especially educational aids and the right facilities for cooperative organization, must be supplied. Whenever, nevertheless, the common good requires expropriation, compensation must be reckoned in equity after all the circumstances have been weighed.

In our own day, the social purpose of private property lies at the foundation of federal programs designed to provide basic needs for the poor. Helping people in dire need is not an act of charity that we might engage in when we're feeling magnanimous; it's a moral imperative. It makes clear the wrongheadedness of the attitude expressed by a prominent Catholic congressman who recently defended his proposals to drastically cut such programs by writing (in an essay published in a prominent Catholic newspaper), "Basic economics and basic morality both tell us that people have a right to keep and decide how to spend their hard-earned dollars."

Neo-liberal economic ideas may claim that to be true. But Catholic moral teaching, including the social purpose of private property and the broader principles of solidarity and human dignity that it's based upon, suggests differently.

The teaching also makes demands on us personally. It challenges us to question our attitudes about our money and possessions and about our responsibilities toward the many around us who live in situations of dire need. It compels us to ask, "What comes first—my Christianity or my capitalism?"

Chapter 9

Preferential Option for the Poor

You could see daylight through the corners and bottoms of the walls of Florence's home, and her refrigerator was completely empty when I visited. Ed and Lorna heated their home in the wintertime by burning cardboard boxes in a wood stove. Kyle took seconds during snack time at the afterschool program he attended because it was sometimes the only supper he was likely to get that evening. Nancy and James were parents who wept with humiliation at being unable to provide basic food and medicine for their family.

I encountered each of these people while living and working, between 2009 and 2011, in the mountains of southern West Virginia, one of the regions of our country most burdened by intransigent poverty. I've changed the names of the people here, but the point is, they have names and faces, too. They are just a few of the folks behind the impersonal statistics on poverty, which are staggering.

Circumstances like I've described are part of the experience of more than 20 million people in the United States (up from 12.6 million in 2000) who subsist on incomes less than half the poverty line—for example, less than $9,500 per year for a family of three! This "deep poverty" is found in city slums, Indian reservations, Appalachian hollers, and places too numerous to mention. And when we extend our view beyond American shores, the reality is, sadly, far bleaker.

Those of us who make up the middle class in America hide our eyes from all of this. We often do that, intentionally or not, by where we choose to live, shop, work, socialize, and send our kids to school. But God hides his eyes from nothing, particularly not from the suffering of his children. Indeed, if the amount of space devoted to a given topic in the Bible says anything at all about its importance to God, then poverty is a problem that is uppermost in God's mind. Consider the story the Bible tells us.

"Poor is the color of God"

When God approaches Abraham in order to initiate what will become a radically new relationship with humanity, Abraham's tribe is a smattering of nobodies. Later, when God approaches Moses, they are worse than nobodies—they are a humiliated and oppressed people. And God makes clear to them that he knows their pain and hears their pleas and comes to free them.

Over time, forming them into his own people, God makes clear the kind of people they must be. Farmers must leave gleanings in their fields at harvest time so the poor can eat (Deuteronomy 24:19–22; Leviticus 19:9–10). Creditors must forgive all debts every seventh year (Deuteronomy 15:1–3), and every fifty years the ancestral homelands of those who have lost their lands should be restored to them (Leviticus 25). These are the Jubilee traditions, with the aim that "there shall be no one of you in need" (Deuteronomy 15:4).

A series of prophets, sent by God, rail one after another against the wealthy, proud, and powerful "who oppress the destitute and abuse the needy" (Amos 4:1), those who enjoy many luxuries while they ignore the pain of the needy (Amos 3:15, 6:4–5; Isaiah 3:13–15; Micah 2:8–9). They accuse the wealthy of having all they have because they cheat the poor (Amos 8:4–5) and take it from the weak (3:13–15; Micah 2:8–9). One of these messengers of God suggests that the destruction of the city of Sodom was not about the sexual immorality of its citizens, but about their proud complacency in having all they needed and their neglect of the poor (Ezekiel 16:49). Another demands that judges be compassionate and fair in court judgments that involve the needy (Zechariah 7:9–10). Again and again, God rejects the ritual sacrifices of his people and calls instead for works of justice on behalf of the poor, weak, and hungry (Isaiah 1:10–20, 58:9–10; Amos 5:21–25; Micah 6:1–8).

In the Incarnation, God steps into the history of humanity in a new and unprecedented way. But the message about God's attitude toward the poor is not new and unprecedented; it is simply reiterated more shockingly as God becomes a poor person himself. And even as his mother carries the incarnate God in her womb, she proclaims that his coming means the humbling of arrogant people, the deposing of powerful people, the disappointment of rich people, the feeding of hungry people, and the lifting up of lowly people (Luke 1:46–55).

The circumstances God chose for this coming are significant. Theologian Lee Griffith, writing of the role of kingship in the Scriptures and the "startling reinterpretation of the kingship tradition" we find in the gospels, puts it well: "The palace in which your King is born is an animal shed. The courtiers and nobility who surround your King are lepers, whores, and thieves, the unfed and the unwashed. Your King triumphantly enters the capital city riding, not on a warhorse, but on a donkey. Behold your King on the cross, bleeding, barely breathing. You want glory? There it is."

Jesus initiated his ministry by proclaiming a new Jubilee, which is "glad tidings to the poor" (Luke 4:18). The values of the Beatitudes he taught echo the Old Testament Jubilee traditions he referred to.

The gospels, particularly Luke, present a Jesus who is attentive to people who are poor. He lives among them, heals them, feeds them, teaches them. To be sure, he spends time with and is attentive to wealthy people as well at times. But while his words and ministry would have been a great comfort to the poor, his teaching could not fail to make the rich uncomfortable. (See Luke 6:24–26, 12:15–21, and 18:18–22.)

"Poor is the color of God," concludes theologian M. Shawn Copeland, summarizing this history.

The Church has always known this. We see it expressed in the well-known Isenheim altarpiece by Matthias Grünewald in the sixteenth century. The artist painted the work for the Monastery of St. Anthony, where many plague victims were cared for. Grünewald depicts the skin of the crucified Jesus as pitted by sores that would have been very familiar to unfortunate plague victims and their loved ones. It is a startling statement of Jesus' solidarity in their suffering.

"A requirement of the gospel"

Much more recently, though, the Church has come to a deeper realization of this reality and has even given it a new name. CST speaks of a preferential option for the poor to describe both God's response to situations of poverty and also the response that the Church and every Christian is called to make as well. We mustn't misunderstand the meaning of the phrase. We are not talking about God loving some people more than others (though Pope John Paul II was comfortable talking about poor people as "God's favorites") or the Church excluding some from its ministry because of their wealth. Rather, like a parent who gives particular attention and care to one of her sick children, those who suffer the miseries that come with poverty have God's special concern. This is especially so in the ways their poverty is caused by the choices of other people and the way society is structured. In these cases, God opposes these actions and takes the side of the suffering poor.

For the deeper insights into this idea and the important demands it places on Christians, the Church owes a debt to a group of twentieth-century theologians who developed what they called liberation theology. One of them, Gustavo Gutiérrez, coined the phrase "preferential option for the poor," and with him several others have offered crucial insights through their study of Scripture, Church teaching, and the experience of poor people in their native South American nations.

In speaking of liberation theology, we have to be clear, because in 1984, a document from the Vatican's Congregation for the Doctrine of the Faith admonished against an overly facile integration of Marxist ideology by some liberation theologians. This left many with the impression of a general condemnation of the entire project. But the impression is false. On the contrary, a follow-up 1986 document provided a far more positive assessment, affirming all of the major themes of liberation theology. A few days after the publication of the second document, Pope John Paul II wrote a letter to the bishops of Brazil in which he described liberation theology as "not only timely but useful and necessary." Just over a year later, he incorporated several key ideas of liberation theology into his seventh encyclical, *Sollicitudo Rei*

Socialis. (The encyclical includes seven citations from the second CDF document and none at all from the earlier one.) The preferential option for the poor, therefore, is one important gift of liberation theology to the Church. It now forms a part of the teaching of the Church's magisterium.

The doctrine refers not only to God's attitude toward poverty; it also means that Christians must take up the same attitude and form their actions and daily living according to it. It is, or ought to be, a distinctive mark of authentic Christian living, a way of life for everyone who calls himself or herself a follower of Jesus and a faithful Catholic.

"We Christians," wrote Joseph Cardinal Ratzinger, before he became Pope Benedict XVI, "cannot choose or decline this option at our discretion. Rather, it is a requirement flowing from the essential core of the gospel itself. Jesus' life is the best interpretation of the motive and meaning of the option for the poor."

In his apostolic letter on Christian family life, John Paul II specifically called upon Christian families to live out a preferential option for the poor (*Familiaris Consortio* 47). In *Sollicitudo Rei Socialis* he wrote:

> [T]his love of preference for the poor and the decisions which it inspires in us cannot but embrace the immense multitudes of the hungry, the needy, the homeless, those without medical care and, above all, those without hope of a better future. It is impossible not to take account of the existence of these realities. To ignore them would mean becoming like the "rich man" who pretended not to know the beggar Lazarus lying at his gate (see Luke 16:19–31). Our daily life as well as our decisions in the political and economic fields must be marked by these realities.
>
> I wish to appeal with simplicity and humility to everyone, to all men and women without exception. I wish to ask them…to implement —by the way they live as individuals and as families, by the use of their resources, by their civic activity, by contributing to economic and political decisions and by personal commitment to national and international undertakings—the measures inspired by solidarity and love of preference for the poor.

Put more concretely, preferential option for the poor means that we should make no decisions without considering how they will impact the poor among us. That applies to each of personally. It's sometimes uncomfortable but necessary to consider the poor among us as we ask ourselves:

Where will I shop?

How much will I spend?

How else do I use my money?

How will I vacation?

Who will I vote for?

What do I do with my spare time?

What career will I choose?

Preferential option for the poor also demands that we're willing to recognize the ways our society and its systems and structures reinforce poverty and make poverty so hard to escape, and then to work to change them. To think that the poverty these people are experiencing this very moment is simply a result of fate, a matter of the luck of the draw, is self-deceiving. Much of the poverty in America and around the world is of our own making, a direct result of decisions that have been made and continue to be made about how we organize society.

A voice for the poor

We see all of this reflected in a remarkable way in the ministry and death of Óscar Romero, who served as archbishop of San Salvador, the capital of El Salvador, from 1977 until his assassination in 1980. Romero's time as archbishop was marked by grave political conflicts within El Salvador, between a repressive government and those who called for reform of the nation's economic, agrarian, and political structures.

As this conflict escalated, a loose network of former military officers and security forces personnel, with guidance and financial support from Salvadoran leaders and wealthy families, carried out a long campaign of politically motivated killings. Many who spoke out against the government or sought to give El Salvador's poor farmers a stronger voice in their society were attacked, tortured, or killed. The victims included Catholic priests and sisters who worked with the poor.

Salvadoran Church leaders had traditionally been supportive of the government and of the privilege of a few wealthy families, while most of the nation's people struggled to survive in dire poverty. Following the killing of a close friend who was a priest by a government-supported death squad, Archbishop Romero became a strong voice in defense of the poor and denounced the persecution of the Church.

In February 1980, he responded to news that the U.S. government was going to provide military equipment and advisors to the Salvadoran military with a strongly worded letter to President Jimmy Carter. He told the president that the actions would only sharpen the repression of the Salvadoran people and asked him to forbid military aid to El Salvador and to prevent any U.S. intervention.

On the day before he died, the archbishop preached a sermon in which he addressed the nation's soldiers and security forces directly, insisting that they refuse to obey orders that were unjust. "In the name of God," he said, "and in the name of this suffering people whose cries rise daily more loudly to heaven, I plead with you, I beg you, I order you in the name of God: Put an end to this repression!" On the following day, he was shot by an assassin as he raised the chalice during the celebration of Mass.

While most of us do not live in circumstances that call upon us to give up our lives in defense of the poor, Romero's witness can stand as an inspiration and a challenge to recognize Jesus in the poor among us and to recognize the structures of sin that help to make him or keep him poor. Ordinary middle-class American life makes it so easy to disengage ourselves from questions and issues like these. It is easy to ignore the unjust systems and policies or simply figure it's all too complicated to understand or even acknowledge. The Church—and through the Church, Jesus—calls us to something more.

Chapter 10

Subsidiarity

There are secrets and there are secrets. CST has been called the Church's "best-kept secret." (In fact, it has been called that quite often, suggesting, I suppose, that we may be good at keeping CST a secret, but that we've made no secret of doing it.) But subsidiarity—at least until recently—has been one of the more obscure and lesser-known aspects of the teaching. Even many Catholics who could have told you the difference between *Rerum Novarum* and *Centesimus Annus* would have found themselves stumbling to explain subsidiarity.

The presidential election cycle of 2012 blew the lid off that particular secret. First, Congressman Paul Ryan, a practicing Catholic, repeatedly invoked the principle to defend the morality of the federal budget he proposed early in the year. Then more than a few Catholic bishops, priests, sisters, and scholars took issue with his use of the term, suggesting publicly that he might need a remedial catechism lesson. When Ryan became the Republican nominee for vice president of the United States, the discussion took on new dimensions (and, to many, new importance). News and analysis from major news organizations offered quotations from old papal encyclicals, and Ryan's grasp of Catholic doctrine was debated by cable TV's talking heads.

If the Church's faith is going to be the topic of discussion on Sunday morning talk shows, faithful Catholics had better be familiar with the topic, even if they're missing a lot of those shows because they're at church instead.

Lowest level possible, highest level necessary

Society is made of groups of many different sizes, purposes, needs, and types. Consider which of these you have a place in:

a family (your immediate family, your extended family, your
  spouse's family)
a parish or church community
a group within your parish community, like a prayer group or
  youth group
a few personal friends whom you join for coffee once a week
a diocese
a worldwide church
a school
a place of employment
a trade union branch
a civic organization, like the PTA or the Rotary Club
a local or international charity
an online community
a branch of the military
a neighborhood
a city or town
a county
a state
a nation.

The list, of course, could go on and on. These groups enrich and improve our lives in all kinds of ways. They help us address all kinds of needs and issues, structure our lives, give us access to important services and opportunities, and keep society humming. In short, each of them, in one way or another, contribute (or at least intend to contribute) to the common good.

With the principle of subsidiarity, the Church says that's a good way, even a natural way, to structure society. After all, consider the opposite possibility. Imagine a single, massive, all-powerful, international agency charged with addressing every issue and need. It might be known as the Commission for Resolving All Problems (CRAP).

Need a road paved? CRAP does that. A labor dispute resolved? It's CRAP's role. A place to learn a new skill? CRAP provides classes.

Someone to talk when going through hard times? Effective protection from international terrorists? Help dealing with that troublesome teacher your sixth-grader is having a hard time with? A way to make sure clean water is coming out of your faucet? No matter where you live or what you need, turn to CRAP!

No way, right? We wouldn't want it, because it would never, ever work. Our families, civic groups, professional organizations, communities of worship, and government at its many levels each have lives of their own. They might not always work perfectly, and sometimes they might get in the way of everything running well. But the alternative —not to have them—is a far worse prospect.

Why? Because situations, needs, problems, and opportunities, though often similar wherever you go, are also unique and particular. People are unique and particular. We're not mass-produced items that can be reprogrammed remotely by an overseas help desk technician checking a manual. Those who are closest to particular people and situations will usually understand them better and usually be most competent to find the best, most effective solutions.

Author James Baresel summarizes subsidiarity well:

Subsidiarity argues that the route to the common good should be left to the most local or smallest level of society that can effectively look after the common good. To the extent that a town can look after the common good, the county should leave matters alone. To the extent that a county can look after the common good, the higher government of state, province, or nation should not interfere.

Note Baresel's use of the word "effectively." It has an important place there, because some explanations of subsidiarity attempt to reduce it to this: Smaller is always better. But that's not what subsidiarity means; subsidiarity recognizes that sometimes bigger is better, too. Sometimes, in fact, bigger is essential. Subsidiarity says decisions should be made and problems addressed at the lowest level possible and the highest level necessary.

Subsidiarity insists that all groups, the big and the small, must participate and be allowed to participate in the life of society in the way they were intended to. The federal government taking upon itself too much power or responsibility is a failure of subsidiarity. But the federal government neglecting to help provide adequate solutions for problems that are too broad, too complex, or too intractable for local governments or other organizations to handle them—that also is a failure of subsidiarity.

We see this latter point reflected even in the word "subsidiarity." It comes from the Latin *subsidium*, for help, relief, or reinforcement. From that root, we also get English words like *subsidy* (commonly used to describe financial help provided to industries or businesses by government) and *subsidiary* (a company that is owned by a larger company).

More important than ever

Subsidiarity has been a part of modern CST from the start. Pope Leo XIII promoted it in *Rerum Novarum* in 1891 (see sections 35 and 36). Pope Pius XI provided the classic presentation of the teaching in *Quadragesimo Anno* in 1931. The passage is a bit long, but every sentence is relevant to today's discussions about the topic.

> *As history abundantly proves, it is true that on account of changed conditions many things which were done by small associations in former times cannot be done now save by large associations. Still, that most weighty principle, which cannot be set aside or changed, remains fixed and unshaken in social philosophy: Just as it is gravely wrong to take from individuals what they can accomplish by their own initiative and industry and give it to the community, so also it is an injustice and at the same time a grave evil and disturbance of right order to assign to a greater and higher association what lesser and subordinate organizations can do. For every social activity ought of its very nature to furnish help to the members of the body social, and never destroy and absorb them.*
>
> *The supreme authority of the State ought, therefore, to let subordinate groups handle matters and concerns of lesser importance, which would otherwise dissipate its efforts greatly. Thereby the State will more freely, powerfully, and effectively do all those things that belong to it alone because it alone can do them: directing, watching, urging, restraining, as occasion requires and necessity demands. Therefore, those in power should be sure that*

the more perfectly a graduated order is kept among the various associations, in observance of the principle of "subsidiary function," the stronger social authority and effectiveness will be the happier and more prosperous the condition of the State.

The same idea has been repeated by almost every subsequent pope, in the *Catechism of the Catholic Church,* and in the *Compendium of the Social Doctrine of the Church* (sections 185–188)—many of them quoting the above passage from Pius XI.

But if subsidiarity has always been important, it may be more important than ever today. In an age of globalization and standardization, when we see the same big products, companies, foods, styles, and lifestyles overtaking so many less dominant ones, subsidiarity acknowledges the importance and vitality of local communities. It encourages distinctive social and political methods and solutions. Subsidiarity prevents individuals and communities from being swallowed up in global politics, economics, and technology. It gives us rootedness, gives us a home.

At the same time, the other side of subsidiarity, the side which insists on a proper role for solutions and intervention from larger organizations or government at higher levels, is also more important today. Even in 1931, Pope Pius XI pointed out, as we see above, that "on account of changed conditions many things which were done by small associations in former times cannot be done now save by large associations." Nearly a century later, it's even more true. Some problems—think terrorism, famine, climate change, healthcare, and intellectual property, for starters—are so big and complex that they render even the best local solutions ineffective.

Not anti-"big government"

Subsidiarity, then, does not offer self-evident support for reducing federal programs that provide food or housing to people living in poverty, insisting that local organizations should handle that work. Indeed, where local governments and nonprofits are unable to solve problems like widespread poverty on their own, subsidiarity demands higher government involvement.

Subsidiarity is not against "big government," it is not federalism, and it is not, as one commentator has recently put it, "Catholicism's anti-statist social-justice principle." After all, the very same popes who have vigorously promoted modern Catholic Social Teaching, including subsidiarity, have repeated time and again their support for some kind of more developed system of global political authority. You'll find this idea advocated in high-level documents by Pope John XXIII (in *Pacem in Terris*, section 137, speaking very specifically the language of subsidiarity), Pope Paul VI (*Populorum Progressio*, 78), Pope John Paul II (World Day of Peace Message 2003), and Pope Benedict XVI (*Caritas in Veritate*, 67).

For each of these popes, there are some ways in which subsidiarity makes government more necessary, not less. I'm not arguing in favor of big government; I'm saying subsidiarity is not, in principle, uniformly opposed to it.

Nor does subsidiarity demonstrate the value of free-market economics. The same popes who push subsidiarity also support strong regulations of the market. John Paul II insisted that "[t]he state has the duty to sustain business activities by creating conditions which will ensure job opportunities, by stimulating those activities where they are lacking or by supporting them in moments of crisis." Are those same politicians who are keen to invoke subsidiarity against big government just as inclined to use it to advocate reining in big business or regulating business activity?

One could readily cite subsidiarity as an important reason for the establishment of a strong national military and also for a national healthcare insurance program. All of these examples demonstrate beautifully how foolish it can be to enlist Catholic Social Teaching as the mascot of any particular political party.

PART THREE

Ideas Into Action

Chapter 11

Family

Home wreckers. That's how early Christians were sometimes perceived by those around them, including by cultural and political leaders of the day. Pliny and Celsus lamented that (as theologian Lisa Sowle Cahill characterizes their comments about Christianity), "the superstitious new religion attracts stupid members of the underclass, as well as ignorant children and women, and disrupts the proper order of household and society by mixing social classes." (One wonders, did some first-century dad forbid his teenage daughter from dating a certain young man because he was a Christian?)

If you consider the evidence, perhaps they came by this reputation deservedly. After all, they were followers of Jesus.

"Suspicion of the value of family life"

Though it sometimes gets lost in all the talk about "Christian family values," the gospels offer us a Jesus who pits discipleship against family bonds and family loyalty in all kinds of dramatic ways. Consider:

- As a boy, Jesus leaves his family without so much as letting them know it in order to stay behind in Jerusalem for a theological conversation with the teachers at the Temple (Luke 2:41–51).

- As Mary tries to protect the family honor by getting Jesus home, he rejects his family in favor of his divine mission (Mark 3:28–35).

- He suggests that biological motherhood does not carry the honor that many during his time believed it did and at the same time distances himself from his own family origins (Luke 11:27–28).

- He calls upon his followers to give up their families in favor of following him and promises divine rewards to those who do (Mark 10:28–30, Matthew 19:27–29, Luke 18:28–30).

- He teaches that being his disciple will divide one's household (Mark 14:12; Matthew 10:21, 34-36; Luke 12:51–53, 14:25–26).

- He seems to recommend avoiding marriage (Matthew 22:30).

- He did not celebrate his last meal with his family, even though it was (probably) a Passover meal, which was, by tradition, a major family-centered event (along the lines of hanging out with family and friends on Thanksgiving today).

- Perhaps most dramatically, he remains unmarried himself at a time and place when religious leaders considered marriage to be a sacred obligation, ensuring that he would be regarded with contempt by those around him.

Given all of this, renowned Scripture scholar Gerhard Lohfink even finds it necessary to pose the question, in the form of a section heading in his recent book, *Jesus of Nazareth*: "Jesus against the Fourth Commandment?"

To be sure, other passages of the gospels certainly do suggest that Jesus had high regard for his own family and the family bonds of others (John 4:46–53, Matthew 15:21–28, Matthew 17:14–20; Mark 7:9–13, for example), and his teachings on divorce are strong statements about the importance of married love (Matthew 5:31–32; Matthew 19:3–12; Mark 10:2–12; Luke 16:18). But you can't read the gospels without coming away with some sense of his ambivalence about the importance or the primacy of family life.

These ideas were not missed by the earliest Christians, for whom faith in Jesus meant a reprioritizing of their lives, moving the center of their concerns away from family and onto discipleship and mission. Theologian Julie Hanlon Rubio writes of their apparent "suspicion of the value of family life," the result of which was that "[b]oth in Roman and in Jewish contexts, Christians stunned others with their refusal to honor cultural norms prioritizing the family."

This is important because when many Christians today talk about the beauty and importance of family life, it's easy to get the impression that the ideal family is a tiny, self-sustaining group that is sweetly isolated from any outside realities that might disturb or distract from what is most important, which is each other. But in a very real way, Christian faith relativizes family life. Being a disciple of Jesus makes one a member of his "new family," the family of Christ that is the Church. And as we have seen clearly, being a member of the Church turns our attention to the world.

"The cradle of civil society"

CST is rooted in the conviction that people are social beings by nature. Society is not an artificial construct that we choose to build because we end up better protected than we would be if we were on our own (as Thomas Hobbes suggested). Living in society is an innate and natural part of what it means to be a human person. Made in the image of God who is Trinity, we are built to be in relationship, to live in community.

The first, most basic, and natural expression of human community is the family. The family is also the first and most formative experience of community that each of us have.

Each of us becomes, for better or worse, who we are largely through the families in which we are raised. Society's well-being depends on the well-being of families. And so Pope Leo's words in 1890 represent well a strong element of Catholic social thought: "The family may be regarded as the cradle of civil society, and it is in great measure within the circle of family life that the destiny of the States is fostered."

Family life is where we learn how to be truly human; how to value, seek, and serve the common good; how to build up a society of goodness and love.

Where we learn to be human

By way of example, let's consider just one context in which each of us are or can be formed within our families in ways that make society better, stronger, and healthier. Consider the progress of a single family meal and all that the ways it can form children and adults alike.

- *Preparing the meal:* Though younger children might not be able to help in cooking the food, even setting the table and getting drinks and condiments from the refrigerator make clear that all have something to contribute and that tasks usually get done better when people cooperate.

- *Gathering for the meal:* From wherever we are in the house, we gather at the table. The one who gets there first does not dig in, fortunate to get the biggest or most of what's there. He waits for the others, even the slowest, and nothing else happens until everyone is there. There is room for everyone, of course; even the number of chairs we keep around the table says so. And when there are guests, there is still room for everyone: We inch our chairs closer together and generously make room, even if it reduces our own elbow room.

- *Accepting the meal:* In our house, it's not uncommon for children to step up to the table, see the food that's there, and immediately grimace or make a comment about what they don't like. My wife and I have insisted through the years that we don't offer alternative menus to please those who are disappointed with what they see; the kitchen is not a restaurant where people select the meal they most want to eat at that moment. Community often trumps individual tastes or desires. We are there together, at that table at that moment with that food, for better or worse, and sometimes that means compromise and settling for less than what we'd consider ideal.

- *Praying before the meal:* Our prayerful expressions of gratitude before the meal help us form "attitudes of gratitude." Though it's usually true that the food was both paid for and prepared by the hard work of at least some of those sitting at the table, it's also true that none of us are solely responsible for what we have. Everything we eat is a gift. When we add to our prayer an intercession "for those who don't have enough to eat today," we also grow in our awareness of the poor and our solidarity with them.

- *Eating:* A family doesn't just eat a meal; it shares a meal.

We learn to make sure all at the table get what they need. We learn to wait our turn in getting what we want on our plates. And in a family, it's almost impossible to imagine the strongest at the table taking the most just because no one else can stop him. On the contrary, we make sure everyone has enough before even considering second helpings for anyone. When one among us is too young even to feed himself, he is spoon-fed. Moreover, the etiquette—saying please and thank you and chewing with one's mouth closed—that is expected from all, and taught patiently as children grow, establishes a fundamental baseline of mutual respect and regard.

- *Conversing:* As we talk with each other, we share our lives and concerns with one another, and the community that is our family grows stronger (usually without our even realizing it). We learn the importance of paying attention to others and listening to what they have to say, even when we disagree with it or when we're less than interested in the topic. When there is disagreement, we learn how to talk about it respectfully. When there is conflict, we learn to deal with it constructively and peacefully.

- *Welcoming guests:* Having guests around the table teaches the value the joy and the challenge of hospitality. Sometimes it might mean there is less food to go around, and we deal with it charitably. Sometimes it means a chance to see that there are other ways of looking at the world than the ones we might share among ourselves, or other challenges that we don't have ourselves. Always it teaches us openness to others, that the community of our family is not closed one, as though we live in a fortress, but an open one, welcoming others from outside the walls of our home.

- *Cleaning up:* By wrapping leftovers and putting them in the refrigerator, in the knowledge that they'll be someone's lunch the next day perhaps, we learn again to value what we have and not to waste it. As with the preparation, we again see the value of cooperation and each person's contribution to the common good.

Now trust me, I am a realist. I have gathered around the table with my family more times than I wish to admit where the main experience is frustration at the complaining or bickering or someone's foul mood. I know family meals today rarely resemble Norman Rockwell paintings. Each meal is like a practice session, where skills are developed, not a championship game, where they're expected to be near perfect. And often this development happens without anyone noticing, because it's something we do every day, habitually, without articulating it or even thinking about it. But all of the above-mentioned skills, attitudes, and experiences are important elements in anyone's being able to understand CST intuitively and live it fully.

And that's just in the hour or two spent preparing, eating, and cleaning up from the meal! Taken as a whole, family life offers each of us nearly infinite opportunities to learn and to live a vibrant, workable alternative to the consumerist, individualist culture in which we live. By the way we spend our time and our income, the things we do together and talk about, the way we address conflict and relate to and welcome people outside the immediate family, our families become, as Vatican II said, "a school of deeper humanity."

Because of the central role our families play in the well-being of each of us and of society, the Church has insisted that government and other social institutions ought to support the well-being of families, through, as Pope Benedict said, "political initiatives that take into account the real needs of married couples, of the elderly and of the new generations." For example, John Paul II advocated a family wage, a salary by which a working adult can support a family without a second parent having to work as well, or, if he or she is unable to earn that, some significant subsidy or family allowance from society.

A family is not a fortress

All this "training" in what it means to live together as persons is necessary because families have a mission to carry out in the world today. CST is not a system of thought to be pondered and admired. It's not a theological discipline only for the experts to tinker with. It's part of the Good News that God offers to all people, and each person and every family is called by him to proclaim not only through our words but by our very lives.

Our families are not fortresses, and the world is not an ocean of acid in which we dare not dip our toes. "The joys and the hopes, the griefs and the anxieties of the men of this age, especially those who are poor or in any way afflicted, these are the joys and hopes, the griefs and anxieties of the followers of Christ. Indeed, nothing genuinely human fails to raise an echo in their hearts," the bishops of the world proclaimed in Vatican II's *Gaudium et Spes*.

Yes, the world has its dangers and moral threats, but that's why Jesus sends us into the world: to bring good news that transforms. There is much talk about a new evangelization today, and each family is called to play a part in that, but if the good news we bring is not "good news to the poor" and if it's not lived out through lives of love and compassion at least as much as it's spoken, then what we're offering is something other than the gospel that Christ entrusted to the Church.

Julie Hanlon Rubio points out that Catholic sexual morality tells us something about Catholic social morality. If the Church's teaching on contraception says anything, it's that marriage and the marital relationship is and must be a turning outward, not inward. Marriage is not primarily a means to a gratification of anyone's needs but a call to self-giving love and service, a call to be fundamentally open to others. Openness to life need not and should not be limited to openness to offspring. It calls couples to open themselves—to children, yes, but also to extended family, to neighborhood, community, nation, and world.

Rubio is simply echoing the teaching of Pope John Paul II:

> The social role of the family certainly cannot stop short at procreation and education, even if this constitutes its primary and irreplaceable form of expression.
>
> Families therefore, either singly or in association, can and should devote themselves to manifold social service activities, especially in favor of the poor, or at any rate for the benefit of all people and situations that cannot be reached by the public authorities' welfare organization....
>
> The Christian family is thus called upon to offer everyone a witness of generous and disinterested dedication to social matters,

through a "preferential option" for the poor and disadvantaged.
Therefore, advancing in its following of the Lord by special love
for all the poor, it must have special concern for the hungry, the
poor, the old, the sick, drug victims and those who have no family.

These challenging words from John Paul II serve as an uncomfortable acknowledgment that the everyday, middle class, American family life that many of us live is missing something important. How can we change that? How can I and my own family engage more effectively with the social matters toward which the Pope points us?

For example:

- Are there ways we can occasionally open our homes and our meals to those outside the family circle, particularly those most in need?

- Are there organizations in our community already doing important work that would welcome our volunteer efforts?

- Are there different ways we could spend the time and money we now put toward our vacations and leisure time?

- Do the ways we talk about those in need (or not talk about them) among one another form our attitudes and those of our kids in ways that are not healthy, compassionate, and Christian in nature?

- Since the family calendar and daily schedule are as much moral documents as the family budget is, are there plans on them that, though perfectly good activities in themselves, could be removed in order to make more room for doing good for others?

Turning my back on my family is not what Christian living is about. When it's lived well, my faith builds up and strengthens both my family and the society in which I live.

Chapter 12

Work

Say what you want about CST, but one criticism that holds no water is that old complaint we used to grumble while diagramming sentences in seventh-grade English, memorizing obscure dates in eighth-grade history, or doing just about anything in ninth-grade trigonometry. You remember it: "This has nothing to do with real life. I will never use this stuff." Unlike trig, CST touches on some of the most important and most personal aspects of our daily lives.

Important and personal certainly describe the topic we turn to now. I can easily arrange the chapters of my adult life by the places I've been employed. My level of relaxation or agitation at a given moment is often related to how things are going at work (which is why I'm such a happy guy, I should add, in case my boss is reading). Work is where I earn the money that pays the mortgage for the home my family lives in and for the groceries that feed the kids.

And CST has some important things to say about work. In fact, the world of work is where modern CST was born. Its foundational document, after all, was Pope Leo XIII's *Rerum Novarum* (1891), a cry of protest against the conditions under which poor workers spent endless hours of their lives. Work continues to have a prominent place in CST. John Paul II's encyclical on the topic of work, *Laborem Exercens* (1981), was, in the words of theologian Gregory Baum, "a daring undertaking" that "raises the Church's social message to an unprecedented height." And the most recent social encyclical, Benedict XVI's *Caritas in Veritate* (2009), has some important things to say about work as well.

The laboring animal

Talking about work means talking about who and even what we are. Work helps define what it means to be human. That's the first point that John Paul II makes in *Laborem Exercens*, and it's one of that pope's contributions to Catholic social thought. Work, said the Pope, sets us off from other animals. Human persons are laboring animals. The things animals do can't be called work. Some might object that John Paul overstated his point, because there are many people who, either by choice or by circumstances, are not employed. But this is to miss one of his insights. When Pope Leo wrote about workers in 1891, he certainly had in mind industrial workers. John Paul expanded the Church's vision of what work is, beyond the things employers pay us to do. For him, work is the activity we choose to do—individually and as a society—to build up our existence, to construct and produce our world, to create our history. Included in this understanding would be activities we don't usually get paid to do, like parenting, learning, or volunteering at a local soup kitchen.

We see interesting signs here of the Pope's personal experience and engagement with communism. The classical Greek tradition that so formed Western society did not see work as a defining human characteristic; for Plato and Aristotle, what sets us apart from the animals is our reason. In medieval society and in Europe of the eighteenth and nineteenth centuries, work was looked down upon. It was Karl Marx who introduced the idea of work as the defining activity of people's lives, though he, too, had industrial workers in mind.

John Paul II, who came of age under Poland's Communist regime and engaged Marxism both as a scholar and a pastor, embraces the idea of the human person as a worker but adapts it to better reflect contemporary reality. In his view, all of us, not just employed manual laborers, have a role in the construction of our own lives and society. This interesting influence of Marxist thought upon CST is a good example of the Church's willingness to draw upon human experience and thought from many directions to enrich its teaching.

John Paul finds the idea of work as a defining characteristic of the human person in Scripture's vision of humanity. Just as this remarkable thinker would later mine the riches of the creation stories of Genesis for insights about sexuality (in his now well-known theology of the body), John Paul gleans important insights about human work in the same texts. In them, we see Adam condemned to earn his living by hard work following his and Eve's fall into sin. Some conclude from this that the need for work is part of our fallen and sinful state, not a part of our nature as God originally created us. John Paul points out that before their sin, Adam and Eve were entrusted with the work of tending the garden God had given them and being stewards of the earth God had created. In other words, the human person is *created* as worker.

Moreover, though there is an element of drudgery to work and the shadow of sin surely hangs over it, we see that work means having a share in the creative work of God! Just as Adam and Eve are entrusted with the care and tending of the Garden of Eden, we continue by our work what God has begun. Here John Paul echoes the Second Vatican Council, which taught that each worker can become "a partner in the work of bringing divine creation to perfection." We should be cautious of how we understand this idea, though, because it opens us to the danger of exaggerating the significance of what we do when we go to work and also of trivializing the transcendent and awesome creative work of God.

John Paul II also argues that our work, in addition to building up creation, builds up us. The work we do forms us, to some degree, into the people we are. This is not to say that our dignity or importance can be measured by the importance of the work we do or that those who do less "meaningful" work live less meaningful lives. For John Paul, each person's dignity and honor is not derived from what they achieve by their work. A bakery employee decorating cakes or a parent doing laundry can contribute more positively to his or her own self-making than an artist creating sculptures or a senator creating laws, depending on the interior dispositions with which they do them. The transformation that happens in me by doing well and with great care whatever work I happen to be doing is more important than any object or idea I might produce. Gregory Baum sees this idea as an important and original contribution of *Laborem Exercens* to CST.

The priority of labor

Still, the effects of human sinfulness surely does mark our experience of work. This is true in the challenging relationship between, on the one hand, the people who do the work and, on the other hand, the resources and processes necessary to allow their work to result in economic value and the people who own these resources. Traditionally, it's referred to as the conflict between labor and capital.

A major principle of CST, and certainly a major theme of *Laborem Exercens*, is the priority of labor over capital: The work people do is never simply a commodity, never merchandise that a company buys from a worker in the same way it might buy the supplies it needs to create its products, and so can never be treated like it is. Persons have a value that far transcends and can never be reduced to the ways that can provide economic benefit to others. Leo XIII had the same principle in mind when he insisted, in 1891, on the need "to save unfortunate working people from men of greed who use human beings as mere instruments of moneymaking."

John Paul sees disregard for this priority of labor in the name of maximum profit as responsible for much oppression and alienation. But unlike Karl Marx, he doesn't see it as an inevitable element of the system. When human dignity and solidarity is respected by all, capital and labor can cooperate successfully.

In CST, this principle does not remain theoretical. It has implications for the real world. For example:

- *Just wages:* Wages are the most immediate way that workers share in the capital that is supported by and results from their work. Wages must be just, that is, they must allow workers and their families to live adequately in modest comfort. Just because a person is badly enough in need of income that he is willing to accept a job for very little pay does not make such a wage just. This, of course, is the principle behind minimum wage laws, and Leo XIII was articulating it back in 1891, when such laws were still mostly nonexistent.

- *Labor unions:* CST has always defended the importance of unions and the right of workers to organize themselves in order to more effectively defend and promote their own interests. John Paul points out, though, that the work of unions is not just to get the greatest possible amount of benefits for workers from owners; a union is not about workers conquering the bosses. It is, rather, about labor and capital existing in mutual respect and harmony. Since the value of unions are questioned by some today and there are even major political efforts to dramatically limit their strength, it's worth pointing out that John Paul II speaks of them as "an indispensable element of social life, especially in modern industrialized societies." More recently, in his 2009 social encyclical, Pope Benedict insisted that the need for unions "must...be honoured today even more than in the past."

- **Strikes:** CST acknowledges a legitimate place for strikes. This is an extreme means for workers to use in efforts to improve their conditions, but it can be a legitimate one in their struggle for rights. It's also open to abuse by workers, which is wrong.

- **Co-ownership:** One possible way of protecting the priority of labor over capital is the development of a system in which workers share in responsibility for the production process and even share in ownership of the business. This might involve workers as shareholders or workers on the boards that manage industries.

- **Government involvement:** Because workers have rights to just wages, safe working conditions, striking, and more, the Church recognizes an important role for government in protecting these rights. Minimum wage laws and various other labor laws are important examples of this.

The Church's solidarity with workers, especially those who work in difficult and degrading circumstances, has been a vibrant hallmark of modern CST from the start. Indeed, John Paul II said that the Church "considers [this solidarity] to be its mission, its service, a proof of its fidelity to Christ."

Chapter 13

Economy

To many folks, bringing up economics for a discussion would sound like a pretty good way of inducing a nap! The structure of the economy just does not sound like a sexy topic. But being bored by economics is like being bored by football—it only happens when you don't understand what's going on in the game. Get a bunch of people who know what the players are up to, put them together in a stadium on game day, and let the screaming begin.

In modern times, there have been two major approaches to the economy, which is all about the way we organize ourselves to produce and provide goods, services, and wealth. The difference between them is in who owns the important stuff, the "means of production"—all of the nonhuman things (businesses, factories, machines, etc.) necessary to produce goods and wealth.

Capitalism is an economic system in which the means of production are owned by private individuals, with the aim of making a profit. In socialism (which developed as a reaction to capitalism), they are owned collectively, by the government or the public, with the aim of making the goods available to all citizens. In practice, it needn't be an all-or-nothing question—an economy could be some kind of combination of the two.

CST does not endorse either of these systems, or any economic system, as the correct one. Rather, it offers general principles by which any system must be judged. No system is perfect and none ever will be, this side of heaven. There is no Catholic "third way," as many have suggested, at least not in the sense that the Church has some specific plan in mind. The Church's interest is in making sure that whatever economic system is used is as fair and just and good as we can make it, in other words, that it effectively supports the common good.

Socialism has not, in truth, had a very pleasant history, partly because of its very nature and partly because a few of the people who have attained power in socialist economies have exercised it with a ruthlessness at times unsurpassed in human history. As a result, socialism is in decline in much of the world today. Capitalism, on the other hand, which is the economy by which the Western world is structured, is in many ways on the rise. It's the world we live in, the air we breathe, and makes us who we are in ways we often do not even realize. For these reasons, in a book like this, which aims to be very practical, it seems best to focus on capitalism.

The good of capitalism

There are many good things to say about capitalism. It has made possible the rise of millions of people from poverty to economic stability. It has allowed many millions to move beyond subsistence living and created the space in which they can engage in incredibly enriching occupations and experiences in education, scientific work, and culture of all kinds.

Capitalism has provided the context for the development of important medicines and medical procedures, technology and methods of communications, the exploration of the world around us at levels both microscopic and galactic. Human experience has, to this point, offered no better economic system for getting goods, services, and wealth to many people.

Capitalism has been able to harness some excellent human qualities—ingenuity, individual effort, and creativity—and directed them toward the improvement of society. It depends upon and therefore fosters some personal virtues and characteristics that are important to human flourishing. These include cooperative effort, inventiveness, innovation, and openness to change.

The papal document that has been most positive and encouraging on capitalism is Pope John Paul II's encyclical *Centesimus Annus*. Here the Pope acknowledged that the market and the private enterprise it encourages have a positive value, and he praised the free market for its efficiency in utilizing resources and meeting some needs effectively.

"Certainly," wrote the Pope, "the mechanisms of the market offer secure advantages: they help to utilize resources better; they promote the exchange of products; above all they give central place to the person's desires and preferences, which, in a contract, meet the desires and preferences of another person."

We must note here what some prominent commentators have failed to when citing these statements (from paragraphs 34, 40, and 43 of the encyclical). In every case, the Pope (who knew well the difficulties of living under a harsh form of capitalism's alternative) closely follows each positive comment with some important and strongly worded qualifications. Indeed, this same Pope acknowledged only two years after *Centesimus Annus* that the Church "has always distanced itself from capitalistic ideology, holding it responsible for grave social injustices." And for good reason.

Survival of the fittest

Milton Friedman, one of the most influential and respected economists of the twentieth century, once wrote: "Few trends could so thoroughly undermine the very foundations of our free society as the acceptance by corporate officials of a social responsibility other than to make as much money for their stockholders as possible." Not a bad illustration, from someone who knew capitalism better and supported it more effectively than almost anyone, of why it is often at odds with CST.

The primary motivation of capitalism is self-interest. As many of Americans learn early in life by playing Monopoly, in the game of capitalism one makes a profit by looking out for oneself, often necessarily at the expense of others. Capitalism has, by its nature, a strongly individualistic element. CST, on the other hand, emphasizes human solidarity and the social nature of persons. Engaging in capitalism means working against that.

The theoreticians of capitalism say in response to this criticism that it's not a criticism at all, because when many people at the same time look out for themselves, the market that their enterprises establish ultimately contributes to the common good. When I look out for myself, an almost accidental byproduct is that others end up doing well, too. And yet long experience shows us that while capitalism helps many do well, it is most often those who are rich and resourceful whom it benefits, at the expense of the many more who are more poor and modest in means and skills.

Another justification for capitalism's individualism is that it treats everyone equally. Everyone is placed at the same starting line and allowed to make of their lives what they will. This account fails to take notice of the fact that, both by nature and by the structures of society that we have created ourselves, there never is an equal starting point. And the unequal opportunities that mark reality provide the context for both personal successes of some and the manipulation and exploitation of many.

Capitalism makes us all competitors with one another. CST sees us all as cooperators. Capitalism creates a culture of sacrificing others for one's own gain, while CST calls upon us to sacrifice ourselves for the good of others. Survival of the fittest is not a healthy way to run a society. It generates a hyper-individualism that disfigures our souls and results in abominable conditions for many.

"As from a poisoned spring"

Avoiding the injustices that inevitably arise from such a survival of the fittest approach is the purpose of government intervention in the capitalist economy. Minimum wage laws and various other laws protecting the safety, health, and rights of workers are all basic examples of such intervention.

The Church encourages this approach, because in a system that favors the rich and the strong, the well-being of the weak and the vulnerable must be protected. John Paul II, for example, called for appropriate control of the market by society and by government in order to protect the common good. Elsewhere he called for "restructuring of the economy, so that human needs are put before mere financial gain." This is nothing that has not been said in almost every document of modern CST that addressed economic matters. Indeed, Pope Pius XI was especially clear:

> *Just as the unity of human society cannot be founded on an opposition of classes, so also the right ordering of economic life cannot be left to a free competition of forces. For from this source,*

as from a poisoned spring, have originated and spread all the errors of individualist economic teaching....

[F]ree competition, while justified and certainly useful provided it is kept within certain limits, clearly cannot direct economic life—a truth which the outcome of the application in practice of the tenets of this evil individualistic spirit has more than sufficiently demonstrated....[The market] cannot curb and rule itself. Loftier and nobler principles—social justice and social charity—must, therefore, be sought whereby this dictatorship may be governed firmly and fully.

The Pope's words here are so strong that theologian Donal Dorr, one of today's foremost experts on CST, points out that they sound more like a repudiation of the foundations and basic principles of capitalism than criticism of its abuses. Many capitalists would agree.

"Slaves of possession"

Besides spawning a harsh individualist ethos, capitalism also generates consumerism. Our lives become marked by the constant consumption of more and better things. This consumption is a need for the economy itself, because in capitalism the only healthy economy is an expanding economy. But it also becomes a personal need for those who engage in it.

In a consumerist lifestyle, we pursue an always higher standard of living. We never have enough. There's no such thing as having more than we need. More income somehow gives rise to more needs and so more expenses. What we're left with is a society in which more than a quarter of the people living in households making over $100,000 a year claim they can't afford everything they "need!"

Consider: The average size of an American home was 983 square feet in 1950, 1,660 square feet in 1973, and continued to rise every year until 2007, when it hit 2,521 square feet. After a brief dip in the ongoing trend, no doubt due to the recession, home sizes got back on the rise in 2011; we're now at 2,480 square feet. And yet somehow, the storage garage business has appeared and boomed throughout the same decades!

Consumerism is poison to a Christian worldview because it trains me to evaluate everything according to how it contributes to my material satisfaction. In fact, all personal satisfaction tends to be reduced to what we can consume. That's dangerous because some of the most important and worthwhile things I can do makes me less materially comfortable and less materially secure.

I've avoided long quotations from encyclicals as much as possible here, while trying to present their ideas accurately, but here's one passage, from John Paul II's *Sollicitudo Rei Socialis*, that demands the attention and reflection of every middle-class American. He's talking about us.

[S]ide-by-side with the miseries of underdevelopment, themselves unacceptable, we find ourselves up against a form of superdevelopment, equally inadmissible. Because like the former it is contrary to what is good and to true happiness. This super-development, which consists in an excessive availability of every kind of material goods for the benefit of certain social groups, easily makes people slaves of "possession" and of immediate gratification, with no other horizon than the multiplication or continual replacement of the things already owned with others still better. This is the so-called civilization of "consumption" or "consumerism," which involves so much "throwing-away" and "waste." An object already owned but now superseded by something better is discarded, with no thought of its possible lasting value in itself, nor of some other human being who is poorer.

All of us experience firsthand the sad effects of this blind submission to pure consumerism: in the first place a crass materialism, and at the same time a radical dissatisfaction, because one quickly learns —unless one is shielded from the flood of publicity and the ceaseless and tempting offers of products—that the more one possesses the more one wants, while deeper aspirations remain unsatisfied and perhaps even stifled.

Strong words and frustrating realities here. So is capitalism OK, or isn't it? John Paul poses that question very directly in *Centesimus Annus*, section 34, which theologian Daniel Finn calls "a famous paragraph that is frustrating for its ambivalence." If, he says, we're talking about capitalism as a system that has a positive place for business, the market, private property, and the means of production, then yes, it's a good thing. But if we're talking about a completely free market, unregulated for ethical reasons in ways that protect the dignity of all, then no, it has serious problems.

In fact, Professor Finn has identified from John Paul's writings four criteria that make a capitalist system also a morally acceptable system (much like, we might say, the Church offers criteria that make war a just war). They are:

1. Economic activity is strongly regulated by government for ethical reasons.

2. Basic human needs are provided to those who can't provide them for themselves.

3. People go about their business within the market in a morally virtuous way.

4. Many groups and organizations operate within a civil society, all working to achieve both their individual ends and the common good.

Let's be frank. These are not criteria that will ever be completely and permanently fulfilled this side of heaven. But if we're going to be capitalists—and perhaps, given the good that capitalism has produced, we should be—we must be honest and realistic about its shortcomings. We must be on guard against the ways it can deform us and always work toward making our world a better place for all, both with the help of our capitalist system and in spite of it.

Chapter 14

Politics

Timothy Cardinal Dolan became the center of a brief controversy in 2012, when it was announced that he would deliver the closing prayer at the Republican National Convention. Besides being the archbishop of New York, the cardinal has in recent years become, unofficially, the public face of the Church in the United States.

"He can't do that!" many cried. "It's partisan! He's endorsing the Republican candidate just by showing up!" The cardinal's office explained that he was simply going as a priest to pray with the people gathered at the event. Then, a few days later, Democratic officials announced that Dolan had also accepted an invitation to pray at that party's national convention. This development mollified some but not others. "He should stay out of politics!" they objected. "A Church leader has no place at either convention." The brouhaha raises a whole host of questions about the intersection of religion, CST, and politics.

In some ways, such controversies are simply unavoidable. Christian morality, and CST in particular, will always sound political, because they have very real political implications. Why? Isn't religion a private matter? Not completely, because politics is about the ways we order our lives together, and the ways we order our lives together have moral and therefore religious dimensions.

The structures we build

This ordering of our lives together—in a word, society—is supported by all kinds of organizations, institutions, and systems around us: local, state, and national governments; the policies and laws they establish and defend; local, regional, national, and international economies;

businesses and the consumer relationships they establish; schools at all levels, both public and private, and the broad educational system they comprise; and so on. Very often, these structures contribute to making our lives more livable. Our society is enriched, strengthened, and protected by them.

But these social structures were not handed down from on high on stone tablets as the divine blueprint for How Life Works. They are created by people, maintained and developed by people. They are expressions of who we are and how we think and act. That means they can be just, compassionate, and sometimes downright ingenious. But like us, they can also be unfair, manipulative, and preoccupied with power, violence, and exploitation. (And, like us, the good and the bad are usually mixed together in complicated ways.)

Improving these structures, developing them, reforming them, replacing them is what the political process is all about. Moral principles help us identify the places where injustice has crept into what we do. And since religious creeds often help us understand morality, it is not uncommon for politics, morality, and faith to overlap in places.

Examples of unjust structures

In some cases, the causes of and responsibility for unjust structures can be difficult or even impossible to discern. In other cases, they are much easier to identify, and bad intentions are clear to see. Many others are somewhere in a gray area in between.

Consider some real life examples that stand at various places along such a spectrum:

- People who live in areas of concentrated urban poverty ("ghettos") are often the victims of trauma that comes with living in the midst of destitution and violence, and this very trauma renders them less capable than they might otherwise have been of thriving in society.

- People who live in a highly eroticized culture are prone to be socialized to value, and value themselves according to, the sexual pleasure they can get or provide to others.

- White people carry all sorts of subtle social privileges with them as they go through their daily lives, making successes and achievements in some ways easier for them than for others.

- School funding comes largely from revenues from local property taxes paid by residents of the area in which a school is located. That means schools in poor areas end up with much lower funding than those in wealthy areas, and so the educational opportunities for poor children are less than those of their wealthier peers.

- An 1857 U.S. Supreme Court decision ruled that black people in America were not U.S. citizens and were not protected by the Constitution. This judgment has long since been repudiated.

- A 1973 U.S. Supreme Court decision legalized abortion, in effect ruling that unborn people in America were not U.S. citizens and are not protected by the Constitution. This judgment remains in force.

- In July 2012, the largest home mortgage lender in the United States agreed to pay $175 million to settle accusations that its independent brokers discriminated against black and Hispanic borrowers. Mortgage brokers had charged higher fees and rates to minority borrowers than they had to white borrowers with the same credit risk and steered minority borrowers into costlier subprime mortgages when white borrowers with the same credit risk had received regular loans. The result was that more desirable homes were farther out of reach for minority borrowers than they otherwise would have been.

The Church and social justice

Social justice means ordering the institutions of society (governments, businesses, and other systems) in ways that support the common good, that the social and personal rights of all people are protected, and that all people are able to meet their minimum needs. Social justice means that human dignity and human rights have institutional and political dimensions.

Fixing the structures that need to be fixed is often the business of politics. It is also often difficult and involves political conflict, mostly because those who have an interest in the way structures currently are, those who benefit from the structures, will rarely welcome such changes. CST has recognized the need for the reform of society's structures since Pope Pius XI's *Quadragesimo Anno* (the first papal document to use the term "social justice"). Since then, CST has left little doubt that unjust social structures are real and that addressing them is a part of Catholic moral living. To name just three examples among many possible:

- **Pope Paul VI** pointed out several structural causes of poverty in *Populorum Progressio*, including the legacy of colonialism, present neo-colonialism, and the imbalance of power between nations (7–9, 52, 56–58). He called for "bold transformations in which the present order of things will be entirely renewed or rebuilt."

- In his first pastoral visit to the United States, in a homily at a Mass in Yankee Stadium, **Pope John Paul II** encouraged Americans "to seek out the structural reasons which foster or cause the different forms of poverty in the world and in your own country, so that you can apply the proper remedies."

- **Pope Benedict XVI,** in *Caritas in Veritate*, speaks of the call of every Christian to practice charity along "the institutional path—we might also call it the political path—of charity, no less excellent and effective than the kind of charity which encounters the neighbour directly." In the same encyclical, Benedict says that the problem of hunger must be addressed by "a network of economic institutions" capable of addressing the sources of food crises, "whether due to natural causes or political irresponsibility, nationally and internationally." He continues, "The problem of food insecurity needs to be addressed within a long-term perspective, eliminating the structural causes that give rise to it and promoting the agricultural development of poorer countries."

We must add here that acknowledging social injustices does not mean there are not also personal choices involved in the reality of poverty and other difficult issues. "Conservatives" usually want to focus on the role of personal responsibility—issues like marriage, family life, and a willingness to work hard at a job. "Liberals" want to focus on the structural issues. Reality is not either/or. There is even a mutual dependence between these two complex aspects of life. There is no reason that we have to choose to address such problems from one direction or the other—except a desire to prop up an ideology rather than actually solve problems.

Party politics

So CST has political elements to it. But whose politics? Which party does the Church support? They're natural questions here in the United States, where the most popular cable news channels easily give the impression that there are only two answers to every question and one of them is always wrong. We live in a highly polarized political climate, and the only people this benefits are those who make a political career of the conflict.

It should be clear from the contents of this book that CST is nonpartisan. It certainly has elements that seem "liberal" or "Democratic" according to today's politics, and other elements that seem "conservative" or "Republican." But the Church is not a party and the gospel is not a platform. Partisan agendas, by comparison, are pale and shallow, and Catholics must have the wisdom to see beyond them. We must reject the temptation to judge the teachings of the Church by how they measure up to one party's platform; it should be just the other way around.

From the Democratic Catholic governor who led the way for many fellow politicians of his party in proclaiming himself to be "personally opposed" to abortion but in favor of wide legal access to it (as if either human life or human dignity are denominational issues) to the prominent Catholic commentator/Republican apologist who encourages readers to avoid reading certain papal encyclicals or at least the parts the pope didn't really intend to include in them (that is, the parts that don't fit Republican economic policies)—attempting to squeeze CST into the mold of today's shallow political ideologies can only do violence, and never justice, to the Catholic vision.

Government protects the common good

In the end, the purpose of all politics and all government is the promotion of the common good. This is the very reason for the existence of government. It is, or should be, the purpose of every political structure, law, and public policy.

This idea has been a hallmark of Catholic thinking for many centuries. Saint Thomas Aquinas, one of the foremost theologians in all of Church history, said the purpose of every law must be to promote the common good. He did it while quoting the seventh-century theologian Saint Isidore, indicating that he didn't invent this idea but received it from the Christian tradition.

Modern Catholic Social Teaching is clear that the common good is state's reason for being. This teaching is in John XXIII's *Pacem in Terris* (54), Vatican II's *Gaudium et Spes* (74), and the *Compendium of the Social Doctrine of the Church*. The *Catechism of the Catholic Church* puts it succinctly: "It is the role of the state to defend and promote the common good of civil society, its citizens, and intermediate bodies" (1910).

The old adage says we should avoid talking about religion or politics —or, heaven forbid, both—in polite company. Avoid them if you must. But CST insists we can't avoid engaging in politics without at the same time turning our backs on living our faith authentically.

Chapter 15

The Environment

There was a time when a book on CST would not have included a chapter on the environment, the goodness of God's creation, and our call to care for it. This body of Church doctrine simply didn't have much to say on the topic. Today, however, any book on CST that ignored the environment would be missing something important.

Recent popes have given the topic some serious attention, and Pope Benedict XVI was dubbed "the Green Pope" for his teaching and for important practical steps (like the installation of solar panels on the Vatican's major audience hall) that have made Vatican City literally the world's most environmentally friendly nation. Still, Catholic teaching on the environment is surely in its infancy.

I suspect Benedict's nickname will one day seem like the one they gave Pope Paul VI in the late 1960s. Between 1964 and 1970, Paul made nine pastoral visits to countries outside of Italy, and since international travel was, for a modern pope, unprecedented, they called him "the Pilgrim Pope." Then came John Paul II, with a list of apostolic voyages that, shall we say, smashed all records. Probably one day, not long from now, Pope Benedict's greenness will appear pale compared to that of a successor, and CST on the environment will develop rapidly.

Papal attention and doctrinal development on the environment will come for the same reason CST focused on the rights and dignity of workers at the end of the nineteenth century and the beginning of the twentieth: a new situation arose within society that produced grave consequences and about which the Christian tradition had something to say, and so the Church had to speak up with urgency. The state of the environment offers similar circumstances today.

How bad will it be?

Unfortunately, much of the public is unaware of the gravity of the environmental problem. Thanks to the efforts of well-funded disinformation campaigns by oil and coal companies and celebrity talk show commentators whose only aim is to score political points, many people think scientists are, as a group, undecided about whether the globe is warming, whether this warming is caused by human beings, and whether it will have a significant impact on life on earth. In fact, people of science are nearly certain: it is, it is, and it will.

Don't take my word for it. In fact, don't take the word of anyone without high academic credentials and a specialization in climate science. Among those who do have such a background, ninety-seven percent recognize human activity as a significant contributing factor to the warming our planet is undergoing (while only fifty-eight percent of the general public believe it) and that the warming will cause major crises for much of humanity. The most respected research scientists and most prestigious scientific organizations in the world accept this as true. A series of reports by the Intergovernmental Panel on Climate Change, the most extensively peer-reviewed scientific findings in history, clearly document global warming, humanity's role in it, and the destructive impacts it will bring.

For several years, scientists have warned us that it's not too late to avoid catastrophe if we make major changes right away. Tragically, we may now be past the "avoid catastrophe" stage and left only to ask, "How bad will it be?" In August 2012, Britain's Sir Robert Watson, one of the most respected climate scientists in the world, commented publicly that hopes to keep the average global temperature rise below two degrees Celsius is now "largely out of the window."

Two degrees may not sound like much, but it is. It will mean the exposure of hundreds of millions of people to drastically reduced amounts of fresh water availability, radically reduced agricultural yields, more frequent and intense heat waves, more frequent flash floods, more frequent coastal flooding, death and suffering from diseases associated with floods and droughts, the gradual replacement of tropical forest by savannah in South America, and the loss of many species on the planet. As we move toward a three-degree rise, these factors become all the more severe.

Because this profoundly affects the well-being of humanity and because God's revelation has some important things to say about it, the Church will surely continue to address it. As CST on the environment develops, it will not be invented out of thin air. As with every other category of CST, it will be drawn from God's revelation and Christian tradition. Ideas that were there all along will be rediscovered, reflected upon, and explored. We'll realize new implications of these ideas that we never considered before and we'll apply them to situations and questions that didn't even exist a few decades ago.

Let's try to imagine the papal encyclical to come, taking its place in the list of social encyclicals we listed in chapter 1. Perhaps it will be called *Sollicitudo Dei Mundis* ("Care for God's Creation") or something with a more contemporary flavor, like *Deus Viridis Est* ("God Is Green"). What might it have to say?

Scripture and creation

That encyclical might begin at the beginning, with the creation stories of Genesis. The pope, whoever he is, will surely emphasize the goodness of the created world, crafted by God, who looked upon creation and called it, repeatedly, good. He might point out that the creation of humanity was one step, albeit an important one, in God's work of creation, emphasizing our fundamental oneness with the cosmos. He might note the detail that humanity was created by God out of the clay of the earth (Genesis 2:7), a profound expression of this oneness with creation and with the planet in particular.

He might also note that God entrusted to humanity the task of naming the animals. Contrary to some past claims that this naming expresses a dangerous conviction about a divinely ordered domination by humans over the rest of the created world, the pope might compare this act of naming the animals to the way parents name their children—not expressing domination over to them, but rather acceptance of responsibility for them, care for them, relationship with them, love of them.

Indeed, the pope might point out that at the time of the great Flood,

God entrusted to humanity the care of and survival of the animals of the world. And then he will remind us that after the Flood, God entered into a covenant not with humanity alone, but with humanity and with "every living creature"—in fact, Genesis says it four times in seven verses (see 9:10–16)! And he'll remind us that the divine sign of this covenant was one of the earth's most beautiful natural phenomena: the rainbow (v. 13).

Here the pope might point out other aspects about our unity with creation, facts about which the authors of Genesis had no idea but which modern science has made clear. He could explain, for example, that our blood is red because of the iron it contains, iron that was produced billions of years ago in great galactic explosions and condensed in the crust of our planet as it formed and from which we emerged. He might refer to the process of the development of life on earth, and perhaps he'll quote Elizabeth Johnson, a prominent Catholic theologian of our own day to point out, "[W]e share with all other living creatures on our planet a common ancestry. Bacteria, pine trees, blueberries, horses, the great gray whales—we are all genetic kin in the great community of life."

And speaking of creation, the pope might point out that God's work of creation did not end with the initial creation of the universe billions of years ago. He may insist that it is a creative work that never has stopped or even slowed since its first moments, and that it continues wondrously right up to today. The universe is expanding and stars are being born and dying. Streams change their course with the seasons as plants, animals, and people all go through their life cycles, always becoming, growing, dying. Creation begins anew with the conception of every new human being, with an acorn's fall to the ground and taking root, and with the planting of a backyard garden.

Scripture and redemption

After considering creation, the pope might turn to the second of God's two great wonderworks: redemption. He will remind us that at the very heart of the Church's good news is the salvation God offers each human person in Christ Jesus, but that Christ's saving work includes the redemption of creation itself.

The pope might point out that in the Incarnation, the second person of the Trinity not only took human form, but, more broadly, took material form, took on the matter of the cosmos (took upon himself, for example, that same iron in blood that was created in stellar explosions), linking God forever not only to the human race but to the cosmos itself. He might recall again the Noah story, which demonstrates dramatically that the sin from which Jesus saves us brought disastrous consequences not only to humans, but to all of creation.

The New Testament teaches it, too, he'll write, quoting Saint Paul: by sin, creation itself "was made subject to futility" and is "groaning labor pains even until now." Along with God's faithful people, creation itself "awaits with eager expectation the revelation of the children of God." The Good News is clear: not only humanity but "creation itself would be set free from slavery to corruption and share in the glorious freedom of the children of God" (Romans 8:21). In Jesus' resurrection, not only are we reborn, but all of creation is. And so Jesus can be called "the firstborn of all creation" (Colossians 1:15–20). Included in the glorious reality we await is "a new heaven and a new earth" (Revelation 21:1).

The pope will perhaps remind us that these same ideas are found in the theological tradition, as when Saint Ambrose of Milan, one of the great fathers and doctors of the Church, taught, "In Christ's resurrection the earth itself arose." And perhaps he'll connect Ambrose's words with the great prayer that stands at the summit of the liturgical year, the *Exultet* of the Easter Vigil, our solemn proclamation of Easter joy, in which we call upon the very planet to rejoice:

> Be glad, let earth be glad, as glory floods her
> ablaze with light from her eternal King,
> let all corners of the earth be glad,
> knowing an end to gloom and darkness.

Taking responsibility

And finally, the encyclical to come will surely connect these theological reflections with ethical ones. It may admonish us that just as the dignity of the human person means avoiding abortion and capital punishment and war, so the dignity of creation means avoiding the things that disrespect and wreck it.

For most of us, the pope may note, that will mean restraining the consumerism that we are accustomed to engaging in so vigorously. Perhaps in an effort to be concrete and realistic, he will offer ways we can take greater responsibility for caring for our world, with suggestions along these lines:

1. Thou shalt drive less and walk or bike more. And when you do drive, slow down, because less gasoline burnt means less carbon in the atmosphere.

2. Thou shalt shop at farmers markets rather than the supermarket when you can. Or better yet, plant a garden. The shipping of foods around the world gives us lots more options but uses lots more energy and emits a lot more greenhouse gases.

3. Thou shalt print on the back sides of paper, too. Set your printer to print on both sides and cut your paper use in half. Also, pay your bills online, cancel your monthly bank statements, and use the backs of scrap paper for notes and lists.

4. Thou shalt use your television, radio, computer, and lights less. And when you're not using them, turn them off. Most of the electricity we use is produced by the burning of fossil fuels. (And besides, he'll add, families should spend more time talking to each other and less staring at screens.)

5. Thou shalt put on a sweater before you turn on the heat in your home, and turn on a fan before you turn on the air conditioning.

6. Thou shalt take shorter showers, and if you're married, a playful pope might add, share a shower with your spouse! Turn off the spigot when you're brushing your teeth. Less water down the drain means less water treatment.

He'll surely also urge us to get involved politically, too, to let our politicians know that this issue needs serious and sustained attention. He may point out specific issues, like the necessity to encourage the development of an efficient source of renewable energy or to demand an end to the practice of mountaintop removal mining.

Having indulged my urge to prepare a papal encyclical (and even whip off a few commandments), I suppose it's time to get back down to earth. If I get too caught up in the high-and-mightiness of playing pope, my family will be quick to remind me that they won't be taking any of my papal bull.

Chapter 16

Peace and War

Thirty, apparently, seemed like a reasonable number. In 2003, as the Iraq war got under way, the president of the United States issued a directive regarding air strikes against "high-value targets." If the number of civilian deaths anticipated in a proposed air strike was thirty or more, the attack had to be approved either by President George W. Bush or by Secretary of Defense Donald Rumsfeld. Less than thirty anticipated civilian deaths meant leaders of lesser rank could approve the action.

What to make of this? Some will see it as a cause for sadness because we live in a world where bad people who try to hurt others must be stopped and innocent people are sometimes caught in the crossfire. Others will see it as a continuation of an evil spiral of violence and a reinforcement of the disregard for human dignity that marks our times. Either way, you don't have to be a Christian—and you don't have to be either Republican or Democrat—to recognize that there's more involved here than just military tactics, that there are moral issues and that they concern each of us.

The Church, of course, is in favor of peace. Peace is good. The question for Christians is not whether Jesus calls us to peacemaking and to avoiding violence; he clearly does. But what ought that to mean in terms of practical decision-making and—for the purposes of this chapter—to the diplomatic decisions of nations? Anything at all? And if something, then what?

"Anything at all?" Some might ask: What have Christian beliefs to do with diplomacy and national defense policy? The answer here comes back to natural law, which we considered in chapter 1: morality is not, fundamentally, a sectarian enterprise. It is reasoning that we can do together, based on human experience. Even national defense ought to be guided by morality.

"And if something, then what?" The Christian moral tradition offers two major answers to that question. One way of thinking goes this way: Peace is good and violence must be avoided, but we live in a world full of people who are happy to exploit the weaknesses of others when given the chance; sometimes only force can prevent this from happening. The human condition demands that violence, though a last resort, remains an option. This thinking is developed in the just-war tradition. A second way of thinking says: Violence is always wrong, and resorting to violence only brings us down to the level of others who use it for their own ends.

Let's take a closer look at each approach.

Waging war justly

The just-war tradition has dominated Christian moral thinking on war and peace for well over a millennium and a half. Rooted in the thinking of Saint Augustine in the fifth century, it was developed and elaborated on by Saint Thomas Aquinas in the thirteenth. It was Thomas who listed conditions that must be fulfilled in order for a war to be just (he identified three of them), while other thinkers who followed him developed the list further. In our own day, the *Catechism of the Catholic Church* affirms this approach and offers a similar list.

(Until the publication of the catechism in 1992, the just-war theory with its list of specific conditions was not formally Catholic doctrine at all, but rather a widely accepted aspect of Catholic theological tradition. Pope Pius XII and the Second Vatican Council had recently recognized the right of nations to self defense, but specific conditions that justified the exercise of that right were never taught formally by the Catholic magisterium before their appearance in this new catechism.)

There are two parts to the just-war tradition: conditions that must be fulfilled to go to war justly and the conditions that must be respected to wage a war justly once one is involved in it. (More recently, ethicists have developed a third part: conditions that must be fulfilled in order to end a war justly. This has not yet been incorporated into Church teaching.)

Regarding just reasons to go to war, the catechism (section 2309) offers four conditions:

1. **Just cause:** The damage being caused by the aggressor nation must be "lasting, grave, and certain."
2. **Last resort:** All other means of stopping the harm an aggressor is causing must be impractical or ineffective.
3. **Probability of success:** The resistance to the aggressor mustn't be irrational or hopeless.
4. **Proportionality:** The harm to be done by going to war must not be graver than the problem to be addressed by it.

Note that the catechism insists that all of these conditions together must be met for a war to be just.

Once war has been declared, Catholic teaching insists that "anything goes" or "victory at all costs" is an immoral strategy. Certain conditions must always be respected in war. Here the catechism does not offered a bulleted list, but does mention (in sections 2312–2314) the principles known as discrimination (noncombatants must not be targeted and prisoners must be treated humanely) and proportionality (condemning "the indiscriminate destruction of whole cities or vast areas with their inhabitants").

Who's to judge?

Who decides whether these conditions are met in specific circumstances? It's an important question, because a few moments of reflection on the criteria above are enough to realize that understanding whether they are being met in any given case is not a matter of doing some simple measurements. There are serious judgment calls to be made. The catechism entrusts final decisions about any war's moral legitimacy in specific situations of conflict "to the prudential judgment of those who have responsibility for the common good," that is, to our political leaders.

In this lies one of this doctrine's weightiest problems. Leaders in the thick of conflict will always be influenced by their own biases and handicapped by the limitations to both their virtue and their knowledge. Surely judgments about whether violence is a last resort or proportional to the good to be achieved depend greatly on the character of the person considering the question. Even in the best of circumstances, relying on leaders who are in the thick of conflict to make judgments about just-war criteria is like leaving judgments about sexual morality up to two teenagers who have already climbed into the back seat of a car. In both cases, objective and rational judgments become difficult.

It's not surprising, then, that the just-war doctrine, while given lip service by leaders to justify decisions about war and make them appear more acceptable, is often simply ignored in practice. Indeed, one of the most obvious facts about just-war tradition is that political and military leaders, right up to our own day, are quick to ignore it when respecting its principles are inconvenient or would compromise their chances of victory. In 1945, it was famously ignored with disastrous consequences by the United States in the atomic bombing of Hiroshima and Nagasaki and by both the Americans and the British in the "carpet-bombing" of the city of Dresden.

Violence is never an option

Pacifism is the conviction that violence is always wrong and a peaceful response to threats is always the right path. Though it is not at all limited to Christianity, Christian pacifists most often are not much interested in grounding their arguments in natural law or framing their convictions in nonreligious language. Their primary concern is faithfulness to the teaching and the personal example of Jesus, who:

- taught that one must love one's neighbor and one's enemies.
- promised blessings on those who make peace.
- rejected "eye for an eye" thinking.
- when unjustly tortured and sentenced to death himself, responded only with acceptance and forgiveness.

It seems that early Christians took this teaching and example seriously. There is no evidence that Christians served in the Roman army until almost the end of the second century. In the latter second century, the great Church Father Tertullian condemned Christian participation in the military and insisted that a soldier who became a Christian had to leave military service.

The fourth-century conversion of the Emperor Constantine to Christianity and the subsequent integration of Christianity into the life of the empire began to change Christian attitudes about military service. Then in the fifth century came Augustine, who laid the foundation for the just-war tradition, which has been dominant ever since.

Although just-war thinking has a prominent place in Catholic tradition and the *Catechism of the Catholic Church* includes it in its account of Catholic doctrine, it's also true that the Church has seemed to be inching closer to a pacifist position in the past half-century. Though the Second Vatican Council did acknowledge the right of a government to defend itself, it also called for "an evaluation of war with an entirely new attitude." In 1983, the bishops of the United States, in a major pastoral letter on nuclear disarmament, presented the two points of view as complementary and both valid positions for a Catholic. That was somewhat innovative. In both *Evangelium Vitae* and *Centesimus Annus*, John Paul II emphasized the importance of resolving conflict by means of nonviolent action.

Perhaps most strongly, the *Compendium of the Social Doctrine of the Church*, in its chapter on the promotion of peace, teaches:

> *Violence is never a proper response. With the conviction of her faith in Christ and with the awareness of her mission, the Church proclaims "that violence is evil, that violence is unacceptable as a solution to problems, that violence is unworthy of man. Violence is a lie, for it goes against the truth of our faith, the truth of our humanity. Violence destroys what it claims to defend: the dignity, the life, the freedom of human beings."*
>
> *War…is never an appropriate way to resolve problems that arise between nations, "it has never been and it will never be," because it creates new and still more complicated conflicts.*

The internal quotations there are both from addresses delivered by Pope John Paul II. Taken at face value, the passage is a strong repudiation of the just-war tradition.

The Church has also come to recognize the right of each person to conscientious objection, to refuse to take part in war because of personal convictions against its morality. This, too, is a development of the past half-century. In 1956, Pope Pius XII taught that conscientious objection was not a valid stance for Catholics. Less than four decades later, the *Catechism of the Catholic Church* insisted on the right to it (see section 2311).

A martyr for peace

In fact, in 2007, the Church received a powerful model of nonviolence and conscientious objection in Pope Benedict XVI's beatification of Franz Jägerstätter. A German husband and father of several young children, Jägerstätter was executed in 1943, at age 36, for refusing to serve in the Nazi army.

He had he lived a rather wild life as a young man. At age 26, he fathered a daughter out of wedlock. But following his wedding to a different woman three years later, a honeymoon trip to Rome had a profound effect on him. He began going to Mass frequently and studied the Bible and the lives of the saints. After Adolf Hitler annexed Austria in 1938, the Nazi government held a vote asking people to ratify this annexation. Jägerstätter was the only citizen of his town to vote against the action.

He received his draft notice into the army in February 1943. At the local induction center, he indicated his refusal to serve, knowing that execution was a likely consequence. He was arrested the following day. Franz's family, local clergy, and even his bishop pleaded with him to change his mind and to serve. You don't have to agree with Hitler, they told him; just serve the military time out of responsibility to your wife and young children, who need you alive. He was accused by others of being selfish and reckless.

Franz's response: "Since the death of Christ, almost every century has seen the persecution of Christians; there have always been heroes and martyrs who gave their lives—often in horrible ways—for Christ and their faith. If we hope to reach our goal some day, then we, too, must become heroes of the faith."

Franz Jägerstätter was beheaded on August 9, 1943. Pope Benedict beatified him on October 26, 2007. He is a perfect patron for us as we resist the temptations to an exaggerated nationalism and engage in the peacemaking and loving of enemies to which Jesus calls us.

Chapter 17

Life and Death

Several issues that directly threaten the right to life itself face society and the Church today, and each of them deserves attention here. Let's turn our attention to two.

Abortion

Abortion is sometimes ignored in discussions of CST. Lists of social encyclicals, like the one I provide on page 34, often exclude Pope John Paul II's landmark encyclical, *Evangelium Vitae*, on the dignity and inviolability of human life. This is a serious oversight. The fact that the two fundamental principles of CST—what I've called the two wheels on the bicycle—are human dignity and human solidarity make abortion a central concern to CST. Indeed, both John Paul II and Benedict XVI have framed the issue of abortion very deliberately and clearly within the context of CST and social justice.

But saying so presumes one accepts that what is aborted ought to be treated as a human person in the first place. We'll consider the question briefly, noting that it's covered much more thoroughly elsewhere. (I'll mention a few resources in the "for further reading" list at the back of the book.)

Life and personhood

You and I started our lives as one cell, a zygote. At that point, we were alive, members of the human species, and genetically and biologically distinct from either of our parents. We were living human beings. That's not a prudential judgment, religious opinion, or political conviction. It's verifiable fact. Scour an entire library of medical school textbooks on embryology and you'll find nothing to contradict it and reams of information to support it. Thus began a process of development for both of us that will end only when death comes.

That fact alone does not necessarily settle the matter of abortion. While living and human are scientific, biological terms, there's another relevant term that is not. *Person* is a word that has philosophical meaning, not biological. Is it possible that a person might be a living, human being, but not a living, human person?

Current American law does not bother making such distinctions. *Roe v. Wade*, the 1973 Supreme Court decision along with its companion decision, *Doe v. Bolton*, issued on the same day, made abortion on demand legal for just about any reason at any point in a pregnancy. The court excluded a certain set of human beings from the protections and rights granted to persons under the law (not even by saying they're not human persons, but by claiming incompetence to decide whether or not they are). As a result, the abortion death toll in America over the past four decades stands at nearly 60 million human lives. The laws of most other Western nations today are similar.

The Church recognizes the right of the unborn child to life from the moment of conception. It offers no philosophical definition of personhood, but Pope John XXIII does assert in *Pacem in Terris*, his social encyclical on human rights, that every human being is a person. The Second Vatican Council declared, "Life once conceived, must be protected with the utmost care; abortion and infanticide are abominable crimes." This conviction has been repeated often by the Church, most notably in *Evangelium Vitae*.

Abortion and human dignity

Human dignity is a crucial factor in considering abortion. Has there ever been a time when our society has made distinctions and choices about who has human dignity and who does not—decided that only some human beings ought to be considered human persons—that has not led to disastrous consequences? Has there been a time when leaving such weighty judgments up to individual opinion has worked out well?

In the Lincoln-Douglas debates of 1858, Stephen Douglas opposed Abraham Lincoln's position against slavery with an argument that sounds chillingly familiar today, though in a different context.

I am now speaking of rights under the Constitution, and not of moral or religious rights. I do not discuss the morals of the people of Missouri, but let them settle that matter for themselves. I hold that the people of the slaveholding states are civilized men as well as ourselves, that they bear consciences as well as we, and that they are accountable to God and their posterity and not to us. It is for them to decide therefore the moral and religious right of the slavery question for themselves within their own limits.

Douglas scolded Lincoln for telling the people that slavery violated the law of God. "Better for him," he said, to cheers and applause, "to adopt the doctrine of 'judge not lest ye be judged.'"

This sheds light on the claim that legal abortion is justified because "every child should be a wanted child." It's true, they should. But 'wantedness' does not describe a quality the child possesses; it says something about the child's parents and society. And if wantedness is lacking, that doesn't alter a child's moral status or rights. We can't justify genocide by saying every race should be a wanted race; justify war by saying every nation should be a wanted nation; or disregard the environment by saying every ecosystem should be a wanted ecosystem. Rather, we insist that every race, every ecosystem, every person be treated with the respect it is owed. "We do not refrain from killing people simply because we love them," writes Ellen Wilson Fielding, "just as we do not (if we are sane and law-abiding) kill people simply because we dislike them. We refrain from killing people because they are people."

Similarly, we would never try applying that logic of being "personally opposed but in favor of legal access" to other issues of human dignity or human rights, including many of those covered in this book. "I'm personally opposed to an employer treating his employees like farm equipment, but he has a right to decide for himself whether to do it; it's a matter of conscience."

John Paul II's words make clear abortion's relevance to CST and social justice:

> Today there exists a great multitude of weak and defenceless human beings, unborn children in particular, whose fundamental right to life is being trampled upon. If, at the end of the last century, the Church could not be silent about the injustices of those times, still less can she be silent today, when the social injustices of the past, unfortunately not yet overcome, are being compounded in many regions of the world by still more grievous forms of injustice and oppression, even if these are being presented as elements of progress in view of a new world order.

How is it still possible to speak of the dignity of every human person when the killing of the weakest and most innocent is permitted?

Abortion and solidarity

Human solidarity, the second basic principle of CST, also helps clarify our thinking about abortion. As we have seen, being a person is never about looking out solely for ourselves with no regard for the well-being of others. Rather, it's a moral response to the interdependence we share with one another. Solidarity is the exact opposite of the cynical individualism that demands a parent can do what she wants to "her body" regardless of what it means to a child she carries.

That's why the ardent promotion and defense of abortion rights by so many people who work to support and defend the rights of the poor and the weak is so inconsistent and a little baffling. In America, the very political party that has admirably and effectively worked for legal protection against all the ways the strong might exploit their strength and social programs to support the most vulnerable has been the party of abortion rights. The party has made anti-abortion politicians generally unwelcome in their ranks and, most recently, has rejected in its platform even the suggestion that we should all work to help make abortions "rare." In many ways, it would be more consistent if the Republican Party—the party that has, especially in recent years, stood for autonomy and self-determination—were the pro-choice force in America.

To be fair, the motivation for the Democratic Party's convictions about abortion has been the protection and defense of women, who surely have been the subject of cultural and legal exploitation and who deserve society's and government's protection. This is a worthy cause. But to support one vulnerable group at the expense of another that is even more vulnerable is surely not an answer. You'll find this conviction articulated and lived admirably by organizations like Democrats for Life and Feminists for Life.

Mary Meehan expressed this eloquently, writing in the journal *The Progressive*:

> *Some of us who went through the antiwar struggles of the 1960s and 1970s are now active in the right-to-life movement. We do not enjoy opposing our old friends on the abortion issue, but we feel that we have no choice....It is out of character for the left to neglect the weak and helpless. The traditional mark of the left has been its protection of the underdog, the weak, and the poor. The unborn child is the most helpless form of humanity, even more in need of protection than the poor tenant farmer or the mental patient. The basic instinct of the left is to aid those who cannot aid themselves. And that instinct is absolutely sound. It's what keeps the human proposition going.*

For the same reason, the decisions of some of today's most prominent Catholic social-justice leaders and CST advocates to ignore the issue of abortion is tragic. Their strident demands that the government has a clear and unquestionable duty and responsibility to protect and support immigrants, the unemployed, children, and the elderly, but that what we do to unborn people is all a matter of personal choice, is terribly inconsistent.

If preferential option for the poor means the most vulnerable among us need and deserve our help and protection, then legal protection of the unborn demands a primary place in our social-justice efforts.

If James Cone's theological conviction that "God is black"—because God always stands with those who are oppressed and shares their condition—has merit (and it surely does), then CST's most ardent advocates can add with conviction, "God is an unborn baby."

"If," as Barbara Newman has written, "it is wrong to kill with guns, bombs, or poison, with the electric chair or the noose, it is most tragically wrong to kill with the physician's tools."

The death penalty

In wrestling with abortion, we face the question of ending innocent human lives. Turning to capital punishment, we must ask, what if the person in question is not innocent, but rather guilty of a grave crime or even many grave crimes? Does his (since most who are sentenced to death are male) own moral status change? Does he, by these crimes, lose the human dignity that demands we respect life?

Acceptance of capital punishment runs through most of the theological tradition and Church teaching. Pius XII, for example, said the state does not take away a person's right to life, but the person has deprived himself of that right by his terrible crimes.

It's worth noting that many such statements come in the form of somewhat occasional comments rather than direct and exhaustive teaching. It might be closer to the truth to say that the Church has accepted capital punishment as an existing reality in society, rather than formally insisting on its legitimacy. The Church has perhaps taken for granted rather than formally supported capital punishment (much like it did slavery for many centuries).

But there has been a strong shift in recent decades. The Church has grown steadily more insistent against the use of the death penalty, and the magisterium has come right up to the line, without quite crossing it, of declaring that it is always immoral and unjust. The reason for this shift is the convergence of two different developments.

First, the Church has come to a deeper awareness of the dignity of every human person. John Paul II, for example, was uniquely clear in describing all human life as inviolable (see, for example, *Evangelium Vitae*, 5)—that is, a person may never be deprived of her right to life—insisting that every human life belongs to God alone (40), and speaking of a duty to "show reverence and love for every person and the life of every person" (41).

A murderer may certainly give up his right to live freely among people in society, but he is still a person. If we mean what we say, to what conclusions do the Church's own teachings lead us with regard to capital punishment?

Is there a connection between regard for human dignity and the use of the death penalty? Consider the fact that the majority of executions that are carried out each year on the planet are done in a few nations that are well-known for their disregard of human dignity in other ways—along with the United States. The nations with the highest number of executions in 2011 were, in order, China, Iran, the United States, Yemen, and North Korea. What do we learn about capital punishment by seeing who uses it most? What does the company we keep say about us?

Second, new conditions in modern societies mean we can in most cases protect ourselves from the most dangerous people among us without resorting to the death penalty. John Paul made explicit reference to this in his historic statement about the use of the death penalty in *Evangelium Vitae*:

> It is clear that...the nature and extent of the punishment must be carefully evaluated and decided upon, and ought not go to the extreme of executing the offender except in cases of absolute necessity: in other words, when it would not be possible otherwise to defend society. Today however, as a result of steady improvements in the organization of the penal system, such cases are very rare, if not practically non-existent.

***

Both issues, abortion and capital punishment, challenge our commitment to CST. Because both are legal under federal law (though in the case of the latter, the law permits individual states much leeway in regulating it) and both very emotional and contentious issues, individuals often feel both helpless and uncomfortable in approaching them or trying to do something effective about them. Still, there are things we can do.

We can involve ourselves politically, making our views known to our elected representatives. As the pairing of the two issues of this chapter makes clear, when it comes to respecting life, neither major party in the United States is without fault, and a party's most effective critics can be its own members. If you're a Democrat, consider speaking out strongly, as a Democrat, to party leaders about the party's adamant pro-choice stance, which is so inconsistent with its values and vision of society. If you're a Republican, challenge your party to consider how its positions on access to healthcare and programs to help people in poverty can push people into situations where abortion seems like the only good option, and challenge the party on its position on the death penalty.

There are other courses of action, too. Support single mothers you know who are in difficult situations. Make financial donations to trustworthy organizations that work on these issues. Pray for all those who are in positions to make direct decisions about abortion (mothers, fathers, doctors, Supreme Court justices) and capital punishment (prosecutors, judges, governors). Attend the annual March for Life in Washington, D.C., in January. Join or initiate a prayer vigil the next time an execution is carried out.

What we can't do is simply accept the way things are, because lives—the lives of people endowed with dignity, rights, and the divine image—are at stake.

Conclusion

What is the heart of the gospel? It is surely that God is love, in fact, an eternal communion of love; that God acts in history to redeem humankind and restore us to the relationship with God we were created to have; and that we are called to love God and one another with all that we are. No mention here, someone might point out, of things like human rights, the common good, universal destination of goods, the economy, or just-war theory; CST must be, at best, a peripheral concern to what the Catholic Christian faith is all about. This would be a mistake.

It's because we're made in the image of the God whose very being *is* loving community. Therefore, we cannot, without doing harm to ourselves, do other than live in loving community. It's because God has saved us and made us his daughters and sons that we must treat one another like brothers and sisters and construct our society in the image of a family. It's because we're called to love one another that we must treat one another justly, for there can be no love without justice.

That is the content of CST. Unlike the platform of either major American political party, it offers a consistent, authentic vision of humanity and human society that calls out the best in us and challenges our favorite presumptions about how things ought to run. In *Caritas in Veritate*, Pope Benedict has written, beautifully:

> *The book of nature is one and indivisible: it takes in not only the environment but also life, sexuality, marriage, the family, social relations: in a word, integral human development. Our duties towards the environment are linked to our duties towards the human person, considered in himself and in relation to others. It would be wrong to uphold one set of duties while trampling on the other (CV 51).*

CST, in other words, is not a selection of items on a menu from which we may pick and choose at will, though picking and choosing would be easier. It all hangs together.

Blind spots or closed eyes?

I talked in chapter 4 about moral blind spots, like the blind spot that kept eighteenth-century Americans from seeing that black people were just as truly people endowed with just as much dignity and rights as white people. Consider now the Spanish colonists to "the New World" who, in the early 1500s, were just beginning the subjugation of the native peoples of Central and South America that would proceed ruthlessly for decades, even centuries. The colonists committed terrible atrocities against those natives and established a vast system of abuse, slavery, exploitation, and death.

One might be tempted to say they, too, just didn't know any better. Times were different. They had a blind spot, by no fault of their own. I know that was my thinking until I learned about the powerful witness of a small group of Spanish Dominican friars living together on Hispaniola, the Caribbean island that was the site of the first European colonies, at the beginning of the sixteenth century, just as the colonization was getting under way.

These friars saw the terrible actions of their fellow countrymen against the native people of the island, and they were terribly disturbed. They knew they could not remain silent. Together they composed a sermon, and they invited all of the military and social leaders on the island to gather to hear what they had to say. On December 21, 1510 —less than two decades after the "discovery" of the New World—one of the friars, Antonio Montesinos, stood before the crowd and spoke the words that the friars had prepared together:

You are all in mortal sin! You live in it and you die in it! Why? Because of the cruelty and tyranny you use with these innocent people! Tell me, with what right, with what justice, do you hold these Indians in such cruel and horrible servitude? On what authority have you waged such detestable wars on these people, in their mild, peaceful lands, where you have consumed such infinitudes of them, wreaking upon them this death and unheard-of havoc?

He went on along these lines at length.

The moral situation was certainly clear to someone—and someone in a position of respect and influence who spoke up strongly about it. So we have to wonder: Was everyone else blind, or were they simply closing their eyes? Would seeing simply have meant too many changes in their thinking and living, changes in society, changes in how they earned and spent their money, changes in the law of the land that were just too big and difficult and, well, too damned inconvenient to consider? Frankly, we can't know or judge what went on in their minds and hearts. We only know that someone who did see spoke up. God knows every heart, theirs and ours, and will one day judge each of us.

CST is challenging, for sure. It confounds our political categories and questions our comfortable assumptions. It pushes us in directions we might not be comfortable moving. But it is also a wonderful gift to each of us personally and to our society, offering a vision that makes our world far more fair and livable to many for whom living might otherwise be difficult.

Let us pray for the grace never to close our eyes, but to remain wide awake and open to embrace what Óscar Romero called "the beautiful but harsh truth that the Christian faith does not cut us off from the world but immerses us in it."

Sources and Further Reading

All Vatican documents cited below and throughout this book can be found at **www.vatican.va**. Numbers following titles of Church documents always refer to internal article numbers rather than pages. Additional resources that were helpful in my own research, other than those quoted directly, are included in the "for further reading" sections for each chapter below.

Introduction

Quotations:

N.T. Wright, *Mark for Everyone* (Louisville: Westminster/John Knox, 2001), 149.

Pope John Paul II, *Centesimus Annus*, 5.

"Blowing the Dynamite," in Peter Maurin, *Easy Essays* (Franciscan Herald Press, 1977), 3.

Pope Paul VI, *Evangelii Nuntiandi*, 19.

Robert Ellsberg, ed., *The Duty of Delight: The Diaries of Dorothy Day* (Marquette University Press, 2008), 184.

For further reading:

On the new evangelization, the *Lineamenta* of the Synod of Bishops on the New Evangelization (October 2012).

The most authoritative and complete presentation of CST is the Pontifical Council for Justice and Peace's *Compendium of the Social Doctrine of the Church.*

An excellent in-depth commentary on all of the documents of CST (up to *Centesimus Annus*) is Kenneth Himes, ed., *Modern Catholic Social Teaching: Commentaries and Interpretations* (Georgetown University Press, 2005).

Chapter 1

Quotations:

Martin Luther King, Jr., "Letter from a Birmingham Jail," available at http://www.africa.upenn.edu/Articles_Gen/Letter_Birmingham.html (accessed July 23, 2012).

Pope Benedict XVI, *Caritas in Veritate*, 7.

Pontifical Council for Justice and Peace, *Compendium of the Social Doctrine of the Church*, 70–71.

Archbishop Óscar Romero, *Voice of the Voiceless: The Four Pastoral Letters and Other Statements* (Orbis, 1985), 178.

For further reading:

J. Budziszewski, *What We Can't Not Know: A Guide* (Ignatius Press, revised edition 2011).

Charles E. Rice, *50 Questions on the Natural Law: What It Is and Why We Need It* (Ignatius Press, 1999).

Daniel K. Finn, *The Moral Dynamics of Economic Life: An Extension and Critique of Caritas in Veritate*, 115.

Second Vatican Council, *Dei Verbum*.

Chapter 2

Quotations:

Pope Leo XIII, *Rerum Novarum*, 3.

Pope Pius IX, *Syllabus of Errors*, 80.

Chapter 4

Quotations:

Francis Fukuyama, *Our Posthuman Future: Consequences of the Biotechnology Revolution* (New York: Farrar, Straus & Giroux, 2002), chapter 9, "Human Dignity."

Chávez quotation in Frederick John Dalton, *The Moral Vision of César Chávez* (Orbis, 2003), 81–82.

Elizondo quotation in Daniel G. Groody, ed., *The Option for the Poor in Christian Theology* (University of Notre Dame Press, 2007), 164.

For further reading:

Centers for Disease Control and Prevention, "U.S. Public Health Service Syphilis Study at Tuskegee," http://www.cdc.gov/tuskegee/ (accessed August 17, 2012).

Adam Schulman, "Bioethics and the Question of Human Dignity," in Edmund D. Pellegrino, Adam Schulman, Thomas W. Merrill, eds., *Human Dignity and Bioethics* (University of Notre Dame Press, 2009).

Gilbert Meilaender, *Neither Beast Nor God: The Dignity of the Human Person* (Encounter Books, 2009), 80–81.

David Hollenbach, SJ, *Claims in Conflict: Retrieving and Renewing the Catholic Human Rights Tradition* (Paulist Press, 1979), esp. 44–49.

Barry Hudock, "Cesar's Choice," *America*, August 27, 2012, pages 15–18.

James H. Jones, *Bad Blood: The Tuskegee Syphilis Experiment* (New York: The Free Press, 1981).

Chapter 5

Quotations:

Pope Benedict XVI, *Caritas in Veritate*, 53.

Pope John Paul II, *Sollicitudo Rei Socialis*, 38.

Maureen H. O'Connell, *Compassion: Loving Our Neighbor in an Age of Globalization* (Orbis, 2009), 22.

David Hollenbach, SJ, *The Common Good and Christian Ethics* (Cambridge University Press, 2002), 130.

Compendium of the Social Doctrine of the Church, 196.

Robert Ellsberg, ed., *The Duty of Delight: The Diaries of Dorothy Day* (Marquette University Press, 2008) 118, 233, 237.

Robert Ellsberg, ed., *Dorothy Day: Selected Writings* (Orbis: 1993), xv.

For further reading:

On relationality of reality: Joseph Ratzinger, *Church, Ecumenism, and Politics: New Endeavors in Ecclesiology* (Ignatius, 2008), 31, 127, 274.

Donal Dorr, *Option for the Poor: A Hundred Years of Catholic Social Teaching* (Orbis, 1992).

Second Vatican Council, *Gaudium et Spes*, 1, 27.

Patrick T. McCormick, *A Banqueter's Guide to the All-Night Soup Kitchen of the Kingdom of God* (Liturgical Press, 2004).

Maureen H. O'Connell, *If These Walls Could Talk: Community Muralism and the Beauty of Justice* (Liturgical Press, 2012).

Maureen H. O'Connell, *Compassion: Loving Our Neighbor in an Age of Globalization* (Orbis, 2009).

Chapter 6

Quotation:

Aryeh Neier, *The International Human Rights Movement: A History* (Princeton University Press, 2012), 59.

For further reading:

Pope Pius VI, *Charitas.*

Pope Gregory XVI, *Mirari Vos.*

Pope Pius IX, *Syllabus of Errors.*

David Hollenbach, SJ, *The Common Good and Christian Ethics* (Cambridge University Press, 2002), 41, 66–67, 217.

Mary Ann Glendon, "The Sources of 'Rights Talk': Some Are Catholic," *Commonweal*, October 12, 2001.

John Langan, SJ, "Defining Human Rights: A Revision of the Liberal Tradition," in Alfred Hennelly and John Langan, *Human Rights in the Americas: A Struggle for Consensus* (Georgetown University Press, 1982), 69–101.

Gerald Darring, "John XXIII: *Pacem in Terris*," http://www.shc.edu/theolibrary/resources/summary_pacem.htm

Pope John XXIII's three characteristics of all human rights is in *Pacem in Terris*, 9. John Paul II's additional characteristic is from the 1998 Message for the World Day of Peace.

http://www.hrw.org/

Jimmy Carter, "A Cruel and Unusual Record," *The New York Times*, June 24, 2012, at http://www.nytimes.com/2012/06/25/opinion/americas-shameful-human-rights-record.html?_r=0 (accessed June 30, 2012).

Chapter 7

Quotations:

Second Vatican Council, *Gaudium et Spes*, 26.

Pope Benedict XVI, *Caritas in Veritate*, 7.

Pope Paul VI, *Octogesima Adveniens*, 23.

Maureen H. O'Connell, *If These Walls Could Talk: Community Muralism and the Beauty of Justice* (Liturgical Press, 2012), 231.

For further reading:

John Paul II, *Evangelium Vitae*, 72, 101.

James Donahue and M. Theresa Moser, eds., *Religion, Ethics and the Common Good* (Twenty-Third Publications, 1996).

Ignacio Ellacuria, SJ, "Human Rights in a Divided Society," in Alfred Hennelly and John Langan, *Human Rights in the Americas: The Struggle for Consensus* (Georgetown University Press, 1982).

Drew Christiansen, SJ, "The Common Good and the Politics of Self-Interest," in Donald L. Gelpi, SJ, ed., *Beyond Individualism: Toward a Retrieval of Moral Discourse in America* (Notre Dame: University of Notre Dame Press, 1989), 54–86.

David Hollenbach, SJ, *The Common Good and Christian Ethics* (Cambridge University Press, 2002).

Saint Thomas Aquinas, *Summa Theologica* I–II, 90, 2.

Leo XIII, *Rerum Novarum*, 34.

Pope John XXIII, *Pacem in Terris*, 53.

Chapter 8
Quotations:

Aquinas quotation in *Rerum Novarum*, 22.

Pope John Paul II, *Laborem Exercens*, 14.

Ambrose in Peter C. Phan, ed., *Social Thought, Message of the Fathers of the Church* series (Michael Glazier, 1984), 173.

Pontifical Council for Justice and Peace, *Compendium of the Social Teaching of the Church*, 171.

Second Vatican Council, *Gaudium et Spes*, 71.

Paul Ryan, "Applying Our Enduring Truths to Our Defining Challenge," *National Catholic Register*, April 25, 2012, available at http://www.ncregister.com/daily-news/applying-our-enduring-truths-to-our-defining-challenge/ (accessed May 5, 2012).

For further reading:

Pope Leo XIII, *Rerum Novarum*, 4–15.

Catechism of the Catholic Church, 2446.

Pope John Paul II, *Sollicitudo Rei Socialis*, 42.

Second Vatican Council, *Gaudium et Spes*, 69–72.

Chapter 9
Quotations:

Lee Griffith, *God Is Subversive: Talking Peace in a Time of Empire* (Eerdmans, 2011), 141.

M. Shawn Copeland, "Poor Is the Color of God," in Daniel G. Groody, ed., *The Option for the Poor in Christian Theology* (University of Notre Dame Press, 2007), 217, 226.

Pope John Paul II, Address in the Santa Cecilia District (January 29, 1979), cited in Gerald S. Twomey, "Pope John Paul II and the 'Preferential Option for the Poor,'" *Journal of Catholic Legal Studies*, 45:2, 334–335.

Pope John Paul II, Letter to the Brazilian Episcopal Conference, cited in Twomey, 356.

Joseph Ratzinger, *Gospel, Catechesis, Catechism: Sidelights on the Catechism of the Catholic Church* (Ignatius Press, 1997), 42; cited in Twomey, 365–366.

Pope John Paul II, *Sollicitudo Rei Socialis*, 42, 47.

Romero sermon quoted in Jon Sobrino, "A Theologian's View of Óscar Romero," in *The Voice of the Voiceless: The Four Pastoral Letters and Other Statements* (Orbis, 1985), 42–43.

For further reading:

On poverty statistics, see Danilo Trisi, Arloc Sherman, and Matt Broaddus, "Poverty Rate Second-Highest in 45 Years" at http://www.cbpp.org/cms/index.cfm?fa=view&id=3580 (accessed August 1, 2012).

There are many helpful essays collected in the Groody book and many helpful citations in the Twomey article, both cited above.

Bruce V. Malchow, *Social Justice in the Hebrew Bible* (Liturgical Press, 1996).

Gustavo Gutiérrez, *A Theology of Liberation: History, Politics, and Salvation* (Orbis, revised edition, 1988).

Congregation for the Doctrine of the Faith, *Instruction on Certain Aspects of the "Theology of Liberation"* (August 6, 1984).

Congregation for the Doctrine of the Faith, *Instruction on Christian Freedom and Liberation* (March 22, 1986).

Chapter 10

Quotations:

James Baresel, "Subsidiarity and the Libertarian 'Small Government,'" at http://distributistreview.com/mag/2012/04/subsidiarity-and-libertarian-small-government/ (accessed June 30, 2012).

Pope Pius XI, *Quadragesimo Anno*, 79.

Pope John Paul II, *Centesimus Annus*, 48.

For further reading:

Vincent Miller, "Saving Subsidiarity," *America*, July 30, 2012, at http://americamagazine.org/node/150588 (accessed March 8, 2013).

David Hollenbach, SJ, *Claims in Conflict: Retrieving and Renewing the Catholic Human Rights Tradition* (Paulist Press, 1979), 157–158.

Joan Frawley Desmond, "Bishop Blaire Discusses the Ryan Budget and Catholic Social Doctrine," *National Catholic Register*, May 4, 2012, at http://www.ncregister.com/daily-news/bishop-blaire-discusses-the-ryan-budget-and-catholic-social-doctrine/#ixzz27WQa3cZ0 (accessed June 14, 2012).

Chapter 11

Quotations:

Lisa Sowle Cahill, *Family: A Christian Social Perspective* (Fortress Press, 2000), 38.

Gerhard Lohfink, *Jesus of Nazareth: What He Wanted, Who He Was* (Liturgical Press, 2012), 204. See also on this in Lohfink, 124–136, 204–206, 227, 253.

Julie Hanlon Rubio, *Family Ethics: Practices for Christians* (Georgetown University Press, 2010), 26, 28.

Pope Leo XIII, *Sapientiae Christianae*, 42.

Second Vatican Council, *Gaudium et Spes*, 1, 52.

Pope Benedict XVI, Angelus Talk, February 4, 2007, cited at http://old.usccb.org/defenseofmarriage/ (accessed July 29, 2012).

Pope John Paul II, *Familiaris Consortio*, 44, 47.

For further reading:

Pope John Paul, *Laborem Exercens*, 19.

David Matzko McCarthy, *Sex and Love in the Home: A Theology of the Household* (second edition, SCM Press, 2010).

Pope John Paul II, Letter to Families (esp. 15–16).

Pontifical Council for the Family, *Charter of the Rights of the Family*.

Chapter 12

Quotations:

Gregory Baum, *The Priority of Labor: A Commentary on Laborem Exercens, Encyclical Letter of Pope John Paul II* (Paulist Press, 1982), 3.

Second Vatican Council, *Gaudium et Spes*, 67.

Pope Leo XIII, *Rerum Novarum*, 42.

Pope John Paul II, *Laborem Exercens*, 8, 20.

Pope Benedict XVI, *Caritas in Veritate*, 25.

For further reading:

John W. Houck and Oliver F. Williams, eds., *Co-Creation and Capitalism: John Paul II's Laborem Exercens* (University Press of America, 1983).

Drew Christiansen, "Metaphysics and Society: A Commentary on *Caritas in Veritate*," *Theological Studies*, March 2010, vol. 71 no. 1, 3–28

Chapter 13

Quotations:

Pope John Paul II, Address at the University of Latvia, Riga (September 9, 1993), *Origins*, September 23, 1993, 256–58, at 257.

Milton Friedman, with Rode D. Friedman, *Capitalism and Freedom* (Chicago, University of Chicago, 1962), 133; quoted in Bernard Laurent, "*Caritas in Veritate* as a Social Encyclical: A Modest Challenge to Economic, Social, and Political Institutions," *Theological Studies*, September 2010, vol. 71 no. 3, 515–544, at 540.

Pope Pius XI, *Quadragesimo Anno*, 88.

Pope John Paul II, *Sollicitudo Rei Socialis*, 28.

Daniel Finn, "Commentary on *Centesimus Annus*," in Kenneth Himes, ed., *Modern Catholic Social Teaching: Commentaries and Interpretations* (Georgetown University Press, 2005), 452.

For further reading:

Pope John Paul II, *Centesimus Annus*, 35.

Donal Dorr, *Option for the Poor: A Hundred Years of Catholic Social Teaching* (Orbis, 1992), 82.

On home sizes, see:
http://www.census.gov/const/C25Ann/sftotalmedavgsqft.pdf
http://www.wral.com/news/local/story/2443194/
http://bottomline.nbcnews.com/_news/2012/06/06/12013928-us-homes-actually-got-bigger-during-ugly-2011?lite
http://www.huffingtonpost.com/2012/06/06/average-home-size-2011_n_1575617.html

Finn, 455-458.

National Conference of Catholic Bishops (USA), *Economic Justice for All*.

Chapter 14

Quotations:

Pope Paul VI, *Populorum Progressio*, 32.

Pope John Paul II, Homily at Yankee Stadium (October 2, 1979), cited in Twomey, 328.

Pope Benedict XVI, *Caritas in Veritate*, 7, 27.

For further reading:

Peggy MacIntosh, "White Privilege: Unpacking the Invisible Knapsack," at http://nymbp.org/reference/WhitePrivilege.pdf (accessed July 10, 2012).

David Hollenbach, SJ, *Claims in Conflict: Retrieving and Renewing the Catholic Human Rights Tradition* (Paulist Press, 1979), 152, 154.

Bishop Richard E. Pates, "In This Together," *America*, August 13, 2012, at http://americamagazine.org/node/150602 (accessed March 8, 2013).

Maureen H. O'Connell, *Compassion: Loving Our Neighbor in an Age of Globalization* (Orbis, 2009), 22.

Maureen H. O'Connell, *If These Walls Could Talk: Community Muralism and the Beauty of Justice* (Liturgical Press, 2012), 25–28, 91–110, 166.

Chapter 15

Quotations:

Pallab Ghosh, "Science adviser warns climate target 'out the window,'" BBC News, at http://www.bbc.co.uk/news/science-environment-19348194 (accessed August 25, 2012).

Elizabeth Johnson, CSJ, "Christ and the Earth: Prepare to be Astonished," 14th Annual Fellin Lecture, at http://www2.benedictine.edu/benedictine.aspx?pgID=2083 (accessed September 1, 2012).

For further reading:

Intergovernmental Panel on Climate Change, http://www.ipcc.ch/

National Aeronautics and Space Administration, "The current and future consequences of global change," at http://climate.nasa.gov/effects (accessed August 25, 2012).

Richard W. Miller, "Global Climate Disruption and Social Justice: The State of the Problem," in Richard W. Miller, ed., *God, Creation, and Climate Change: A Catholic Response to the Environmental Crisis* (Orbis, 2010), 1–34.

Pope John Paul II's 1990 World Day of Peace Message, "Peace With God the Creator, Peace With All Creation."

Pope Benedict XVI, *Caritas in Veritate*, 43–52.

Pope Benedict XVI, 2010 World Day of Peace Message, "If You Want to Cultivate Peace, Protect Creation."

Drew Christiansen and Walter Grazer, eds., *"And God Saw That It Was Good": Catholic Theology and the Environment* (United States Catholic Conference, 1996).

http://www.chasinggreen.org/

http://www.justlivegreener.com/

http://www.50waystohelp.com/

Chapter 16

Quotations:

Second Vatican Council, *Gaudium et Spes*, 78.

Pontifical Council for Justice and Peace, *Compendium of the Social Doctrine of the Church*, 496.

For further reading:

Mark Benjamin, "When Is an Accidental Civilian Death Not an Accident?" *Salon*, July 30, 2012, at http://www.salon.com/2007/07/30/collateral_damage/ (accessed August 12, 2012).

Lisa Sowle Cahill, *Love Your Enemies: Discipleship, Pacifism, and Just War Theory* (Augsburg Fortress Press, 1994).

John Howard Yoder, *The War of the Lamb: The Ethics of Nonviolence and Peacemaking* (Brazos, 2009).

Jean Bethke, *But Was It Just? Reflections on the Morality of the Persian Gulf War* (Doubleday, 1992).

Robert W. Brimlow, *What About Hitler? Wrestling With Jesus's Call to Nonviolence in an Evil World* (Brazos Press, 2006).

William Doino, Jr., "Franz Jägerstätter: Martyr and Model," On The Square blog, October 25, 2007, at http://www.firstthings.com/onthesquare/2007/10/franz-jgersttter-martyr-and-mo (accessed September 12, 2012).

National Conference of Catholic Bishops (USA), *The Challenge of Peace*.

Chapter 17

Quotations:

Second Vatican Council, *Gaudium et Spes*, 51.

Lincoln–Douglas debate quotations cited in Ann Conlon, ed., *The Debate Since Roe: Making the Case Against Abortion* (1975-2010) (Human Life Review, 2010), 158, 77–78.

Ellen Wilson Fielding in Conlon, 79.

Pope John Paul II, *Evangelium Vitae*, 5, 20, 56.

Mary Meehan in Conlon, 263.

Barbara Newman in Conlon, 263.

For further reading:

http://www.feministsforlife.org/

Simon Rogers, "Death Penalty Statistics, Country by Country," *The Guardian*, Data Blog, at http://www.guardian.co.uk/news/datablog/2011/mar/29/death-penalty-countries-world (accessed August 13, 2012).

Francis J. Beckwith, *Defending Life: A Moral and Legal Case Against Abortion* (Cambridge University Press, 2007).

Hadley Arkes, *Natural Rights and the Right to Choose* (Cambridge University Press, 2004).

Conclusion

Pope Benedict XVI, *Caritas in Veritate*, 51.

Montesinos sermon in Gustavo Gutiérrez, *Las Casas: In Search of the Poor of Jesus Christ* (Wipf & Stock Publishers, 2002), 27–31.

Archbishop Óscar Romero, *Voice of the Voiceless: The Four Pastoral Letters and Other Statements* (Orbis, 1985), 178.

Happy the People
When Loves Becomes Justice

ISBN: 9780764-822339

Justice has always been a fundamental concern of the Church, yet many Catholics are only vaguely aware of the Church's teachings on social justice. Happy the People, uses teaching documents, Scripture and examples to teach readers, not only about social teachings, but why it is important to recognize their interconnection to our lives.

Along the Way
Lessons for an Authentic Journey of Faith

ISBN: 9780764-821646

Catholic life is not easy, especially in our contemporary society that views Christian beliefs in subjective and relativistic terms. As Christians, we cannot simply stand on the sidelines and watch. Along the Way, presents hot button Catholic topics such as materialism, life issues, reconciliation, charity and much more.